New Jihadists & Islam

NEW JIHADISTS & ISLAM

DANIEL (GHASEM) AKBARI

Copyright © 2013 Daniel (Ghasem) Akbari.

All rights reserved. No part of this book may be reproduced, stored, or transmitted by any means—whether auditory, graphic, mechanical, or electronic—without written permission of both publisher and author, except in the case of brief excerpts used in critical articles and reviews. Unauthorized reproduction of any part of this work is illegal and is punishable by law.

ISBN: 978-1-4834-0275-8 (sc)
ISBN: 978-1-4834-0274-1 (e)

Because of the dynamic nature of the Internet, any web addresses or links contained in this book may have changed since publication and may no longer be valid. The views expressed in this work are solely those of the author and do not necessarily reflect the views of the publisher, and the publisher hereby disclaims any responsibility for them.

Any people depicted in stock imagery provided by Thinkstock are models, and such images are being used for illustrative purposes only.
Certain stock imagery © Thinkstock.

Lulu Publishing Services rev. date: 08/19/2013

For Azeizaye Delam

TABLE OF CONTENTS

Acknowledgments ix
Foreword... xi
Chapter 1   The New Generation of Terrorists in the United
            States 1
Chapter 2   The Cost of Standing for Truth 11
Chapter 3   Important Islamic sources 15
Chapter 4   Islam and Jihad 22
Chapter 5   Who is a Sheikh?.. 34
Chapter 6   Different Attitudes Toward Jihad Among Muslims
            Who Live in the West 47
Chapter 7   Suicide terrorism 58
Chapter 8   Evangelical Christians and Islam 63
Glossary 77
Bibliography 83

Acknowledgments

My special thanks go to Paul Tetreault for editing this book and for all the years he spent to improve my English. I have always admired his knowledge about every aspect of life. His has always been like a brother for me and knowing him is an honor for me. He is an Islamic scholar who has never tried to show off his knowledge in this area. I also thank the Robinson's who are like our parents. We live in this free country because of them. They treated us like their children and supported us to get established. I can publish this book because of the blessing of freedom of speech. Without the Robinson's we would have missed this opportunity. I just say "Sizi Seviyoruz."

Foreword

Steaming in from sea up the narrow channel of the Piscataqua River, with New Hampshire to port and Maine to starboard, you can't miss "Alcatraz of the East," the gray stone castle of Portsmouth Naval Prison. The old gray ghost looms broodingly atop a small hill at the southwest tip of Seavey Island. For over two hundred years the island has been home to Portsmouth Naval Shipyard and some the most resourceful, dedicated, and ingenious craftsmen who ever crossed the quarterdeck of a U.S. Navy ship or sub. Ayup. The prison was built on the island because, at Portsmouth, the Piscataqua has one of the largest tidal ranges and fastest tidal currents of any river in North America. The fast current explains the name of the next landmark a few hundred yards up the channel on the southeast tip of the island, "pull and be damned point." The name survives from the days before powered tugs when crews in longboats rowed sailing ships up channel. If delays or mistakes caused the tow to miss slack water, all the oarsmen could do was "pull and be damned!"

Steaming midway between the prison and the point, you're directly south of a large pond on the island. It's in this pond, so the story goes, that the timber used to repair the hull planking on the world's oldest commissioned warship, the *USS Constitution*, must soak and weather for at least ten years. These planks are very special, they're responsible for *Constitution's* nickname, "Old Ironsides," earned as her crew rejoiced when enemy canon balls, hitting broadside, bounced harmlessly off.

For their time, *Constitution* and her sister ships were outrageously expensive, ultra high-tech weapons systems, more heavily gunned than ships their size and faster than ships with equivalent armament. They were built for just one purpose, to defeat the threat to the United States from Islamic terrorists that arose six years before the real Constitution—the one written on parchment—was even ratified by all 13 states. Most people don't know it, but the first Islamic attack against the United States took place not in 2001 or 1968 but in March, 1783, when two American ships transiting the Mediterranean were pursued by nine Algerian corsairs. A year later, in 1784, the brig *Betsey* was captured in the Atlantic by corsairs from Morocco. *Betsey* was not the first ship from the American colonies to be captured—Islamic attacks against American ships date back to the 1600s—but she was the first ship of the new United States to be captured by Muslims. She was captured by Morocco, a North African client state along with Tripoli, Tunis, and Algiers, of the Islamic Ottoman Empire. Muslims call North Africa the *Mahgreb*, Arabic for "sunset," since Africa is west of Arabia. We call it Barbary for the native Berber people, Christians who were conquered by Muslim warriors sweeping out of Arabia in what history knows as the First Jihad. We also have a name for terrorists operating on the high seas, we call them pirates.

As Joshua London has documented in his excellent book <u>Victory in Tripoli: How America's War with the Barbary Pirates Established the U.S. Navy and Built a Nation</u>, the *Betsey's* capture was part of *al-jihad fi'l bahr*, the Holy War at sea, that lasted from the 16th through the 18th centuries. Slavery is legal in Islam, and this Jihad saw countless non-Muslim sailors swept into the misery of the Islamic slave trade. The fortunate were held for ransom. The profits of human trafficking together with the treasure captured as booty—the fruits of Jihad and a technical legal concept in Sharia—or extorted to ransom vessels and sailors made piracy the principal industry and chief source of revenue for the Barbary regencies. The year following *Betsey's* capture two more U.S. ships, *Dauphin* and *Maria,* were seized by Algiers and their crews enslaved. In 1786, Thomas Jefferson and John Adams, who were then in Europe, attempted to open negotiations with the Barbary states. They asked Tripoli's ambassador to Britain the obvious question, why the Barbary states were making war on the U.S. when the U.S. had done nothing to provoke hostilities. The answer they received and transmitted back to the Continental Congress was ominous, and has become the most important issue of the 21st century:

> That it was founded on the Laws of their Prophet, that it was written in their Koran, that all nations who should not have acknowledged their authority were sinners, that it was their right and duty to make war upon them wherever they could be found, and to make slaves of all they could take as Prisoners, and that every Musselman who should be slain in Battle was sure to go to Paradise.

The ambassador couched his answer in phrases taken directly from Koran that you will find explained in the pages of this book.

For the next 15 years the U.S. followed a policy of appeasement, paying ransom money and tribute and even giving arms to the Muslim terrorists. By 1794 it was clear to George Washington that the only way to end the terrorism was to defeat the terrorists in war. Congress passed the Naval Armament Act, providing for the construction of *Constitution* and her sister ships. In 1801, Tripoli demanded increased tribute payments. When now President Thomas Jefferson refused, Tripoli declared war against the U.S. Jefferson responded by sending the Navy to fight the U.S.'s first foreign war, known to history as the First Barbary War. Hostilities raged from 1801 to 1805, with *Constitution* joining the fray as flagship of the

Mediterranean squadron in 1803. The war ended with the U.S. abandoning an ally, the Pasha of Tripoli's brother, and plans for regime change in order to obtain a treaty and ransom 300 American hostages. The war left a lasting legacy on the U.S. Navy, particularly the Marine Corps. The familiar phrase "to the shores of Tripoli" in the Marines' Hymn comes from this war, as does as the shape and name of the Marine Officer's sword, the Mameluke, honoring a particular band of Jihadis. Even the nickname "Leathernecks" comes from the Marines' practical response to verse 4 of chapter 47 of Koran, which commands Muslims to "smite the necks of unbelievers until you have killed and wounded many of them." The Marines defended against this tactic with thick leather collars, hence the name "Leathernecks."

The treaty did not end the Barbary practice of taking American ships and seamen hostage. With Europe mired in the Napoleonic Wars and England and the U.S. distracted by the War of 1812 there were no resources to police the Muslims. Finally, in 1815, at President James Madison's urging, Congress once again sent the Navy to war. Commodore Stephen Decatur, hailed by no less than Admiral Lord Nelson for his skill and daring in the First Barbary War, quickly captured two Algerine ships to use as bargaining chips and, with the threat of the arrival of a second squadron of U.S. Navy ships under the command of William Bainbridge, was able to bring Algiers to terms.

America responded effectively to Islamic terrorism in the Barbary Wars. While Washington, Adams, Jefferson, and Madison did not eliminate the threat posed by Islam's teachings, history shows they assessed the threat honestly and, therefore, accurately. Their actions were effective to prevent terrorism from reaching our shores or continuing to endanger American interests and, it should be mentioned, Americans were up to the task as well. It is not overstatement to say that Islamic Jihad is the reason there is a U.S. Navy, and the proof of that fact, America's oldest war memorial, sits just off Decatur Road—named for Stephen Decatur—behind Preble Hall—named for the commander of the Mediterranean Squadron during the First Barbary War—on the yard of the U.S. Naval Academy.

Today we live in a time when truth has fallen to the ground and information about almost every subject has become political. This book marks the arrival of a fresh new voice on the side of telling the truth about Islam, Daniel Akbari. He arrives with credentials and experience unequaled by *any* currently active Western writer. He is an Islamic *mujtahid*—scholar—who has lived most of his life in one of the two nations on earth that follow Islam most correctly. As a mujtahid, he reads Classical Arabic, has comprehensive knowledge of the Koran, Hadith, and Sira, and is trained in *usul-al-fiqh*, the techniques of legal reasoning used by Islamic scholars to harmonize seemingly contradictory passages in Islam's authoritative documents and make judgments on Islamic law. In other words, he is competent to perform *ijtihad*. The gates of ijtihad are closed on issues on which scholars have reached consensus, but there is an ongoing need for ijtihad on subjects not covered by previous rulings, particularly in courtroom situations.

Mujtahids typically follow one of three career patterns. They become leaders in a mosque, professors in Islamic seminaries, or Sharia law lawyers *(wakil)* and judges *(qadi)*. Most people don't have an accurate picture of Sharia law. If we think about it at all we think it must be similar to Western law, but imagine you got a traffic ticket, were charged with making war against God, and your lawyer shows up at court to defend you with his Bible. A thousand years ago in the West, courts were church courts, lawyers and judges were Catholic priests, and the Bible was the ultimate source of law. In the Islamic world, that situation has never changed. Sharia is not just a legal system that is tangential to the lives of most citizens; it is the rules for how to correctly practice Islam. It dictates every aspect of life from cradle to grave and applies to every form of human interaction. Daniel Akbari chose the third path. He is a Number One Wakil, certified to handle death penalty cases and admitted to practice before his country's Supreme Court.

No matter how much you know about Islam you will find something new in the pages of this book. By far the most important information is that Islam is goal driven, not rule driven. Islam has a default set of moral rules that are nothing like the Judeo-Christian moral rules on which Western liberty is based. They either allow things Western rules prohibit or do not apply to everybody equally. But Islam's default rules can all be set aside to achieve the *maqassid-al-sharia*, Islam's ultimate goals. The most important of these is that Muslims must fight non-Muslims until the religion of Allah reigns supreme. *Anyone* who comes to believe in this goal is a potential Jihadi, regardless of whatever Islamic rules he or she keeps or ignores. We're blessed to have Daniel Akbari to explain that, and many other things, to us.

Paul J. Tetreault, Jr., Esq.
Commander, USNR (ret.)
04 July 2013

CHAPTER ONE

THE NEW GENERATION OF TERRORISTS IN THE UNITED STATES

When the Boston Marathon bombing suspect Dzhokhar Tsarnaev told investigators he and his brother Tamerlan were not directed by any foreign terrorist organizations, the U.S security system should have recognized their attack as a new type of terrorism, much harder to combat than terrorism directed by known jihadi organizations like Al-Qaida. U.S citizens have the right to expect their security system to accurately analyze the cause of terrorist attacks, so U.S. security analysts need to notice the differences between the Boston Marathon bombing and attacks like 9/11. The purpose of this book is to fill that need by describing the motivations, methods, and characteristics of this next wave of jihadists.

We should question how the Department of Homeland Security—a gigantic security establishment—left us so vulnerable to an attack like the Boston bombing. To answer this question we need to know who these terrorists really are and why they commit these horrible acts and then discuss the root of the vulnerability of the security system. There are various groups of security experts who have different opinions about what makes one a terrorist. Discussing all forms of terrorism is not the main issue in the present book. This book specifically pertains to a new form of Islamic jihad in the United States. By and large, Americans are familiar with the term *jihad*. Since jihad is an Islamic term that needs to be operationally defined, discussing Islamic ideas about it is inevitable. At first glance using the term jihad might seem irrelevant to the Boston Marathon bombing but, after you become familiar with the theory of the new generation of jihadists, it will be easier to see the connections.

Even though many authors have already written about Jihad, this book is quite different than them for the following reasons:

1. The Islamic sources that have been used as the references are credible and accepted by the most well-known Islamic schools.
2. We analyze a new generation of jihadists who are entirely different than what has already been discussed by other authors.
3. The method of analyzing Islamic books and Western articles and books is legal reasoning from the stand point of a sharia lawyer[1]

Terrorism and Jihad

There are tons of books and articles that have defined terrorism. Even though some of them have done a very good job categorizing different types of terroristic attacks, the majority don't bother to mention the differences between assassination and terror. Nowadays in political science, assassination is counted as a terroristic act. But in this book, we do not put assassination in the same category with terror to avoid any confusion that might arise from using them as equivalent concepts. Some authors in the area of political science have defined assassination as killing the head of a state or other state officials (Combs, 1997 p. 20). The purpose of assassination is to eliminate a state official who is considered to be an impediment in the way of the assassin's desired goals. Even though assassinating a state official might scare other state officials, creating fear is not the direct purpose of the assassination but just a collateral effect. Conversely, the primary goal of a terroristic act is to frighten the members of a society to achieve a political goal. Terrorism is also defined as a "politically motivated violence perpetrated by individuals, groups, or state-sponsored agents, intended to instill feelings of terror and helplessness in a population in order to influence decision making and to change behavior." (Fathali M. Moghaddam). This definition excludes beliefs and religions as the motivation for terroristic acts, which makes the definition incomplete. A terrorist in one's perspective might be somebody else's hero and that's probably why Bin Ladan's corpse was thrown into the ocean. If he had been buried in a known place he might have been worshiped by those for whom he was a hero. Another example would be the burial process for the Boston Marathon bomber who was killed. He was buried anonymously for the same reason.

Another difference between assassination and a terroristic act relates to choosing the target. Unlike assassination, in a terroristic act the targets may be innocent, apolitical civilians. Terrorists do not try to distinguish between innocent or perceived guilty people. They just think about carrying out their mission and subjugating the people of the target society. Since our focus in this book is Jihadists, we will not discuss assassination, which is mostly a political phenomenon.

There are four assumptions we can make about Western academics who write about terrorism. One of them is that they are afraid of getting killed for what they write about the connection between Islam and terrorism. The second assumption is that they want to discourage Muslims from more terroristic attacks by misleading them about what Islam actually teaches. The third assumption—and it really isn't an assumption because it is obvious from what they write—is that they themselves don't know that Islam has something to do with terrorism. The last assumption is that they want to gain the approval of so-called "moderate Muslims."

Those authors who want to avoid the danger of getting assassinated really don't have anything to worry about because jihadists would not kill them for telling the truth about Jihad. Jihadists are proud of being called the true Muslims who know that Jihad is one of the most important duties for a Muslim. As Abd al-Salam Faraj—one of the primary influences on the Muslim Brothers who assassinated Anwar Sadat—said in his book The Absent Obligation, "Jihad is a duty as important as other Islamic pillars." (Benjamin Netanyahu)

There is no doubt that Jihadi attacks are the dominant type of terrorism in the United States. It is also apparent that jihad is an Islamic term. So it is suspicious that Western academic authors who write about terrorism all claim that jihad has nothing to do with religion. Normally in academia, specifically in criminology, scholars almost never agree about the root cause of a phenomenon so this consensus that jihad has nothing to do with religion can properly be called the miracle of the 21st century. Since believing in miracles is taboo in science and academic writing, we need the assumptions listed above to help solve this mystery.

In scientific writing, authors should support their assertions with credible documents. But when analyzing the roots of jihad, Western academics seem reluctant to be meticulous in their analyses. Rather than quoting Islamic sources, they make conclusory assertions like, "Islam is not, in any sense, a violent religion." (Combs, 1997), or "the religious code permits neither suicide nor the terrorizing of innocent people" (Bandura, A. 1990). The consensus among Western academics that Islam is not violent, supported only by conclusory assertions, is most abnormal and quite unscholarly. It not only flies in the face of what the terrorists themselves explain is their motivation, but also begs the questions of on what basis these academics can claim to be so expert in the teachings of Islam that they can advance assertions unsupported by documentary evidence. To be competent to render a ruling on the teachings of Islam—to be qualified to "judge of its codes"—demands a very specific skill set established by Islam itself. One must have 1) a comprehensive knowledge of the Islamic sources, including Koran, Sira, and Hadith, 2) a command of the classical Arabic language as used in the authoritative documents, and 3) a comprehensive understanding of "usul-al-fiqh," the tools and methods of analytical reasoning used by Muslim scholars to interpret and harmonize the authoritative documents. The conclusory assertions made by Western academics that Islam has nothing to do with jihad are neither scientific nor reasonable and cannot be justified simply by having the title of professor at a prestigious university. A professor from a high ranking university is expected to cite authorities to justify his assertions. The magic secret that allows these "experts" on terrorism to analyze the whole corpus of Islamic teachings in one sentence is a phenomenon that needs to be shared, because with it we could undoubtedly understand all legal systems in less than an hour. Wouldn't that be something?

If you pick a book about terrorism at random, you will see there are repeated concepts like, "radicals," "fanatics," "extremists," and so on. All the Western academic writers use these terms but, for unknown reasons, nobody has defined them to make it clear what they mean.

Who is a radical, fanatic, or extremist? Is he the one who misinterprets the sources of his belief? Is he the one who wants to take every bit of his belief seriously? Are extremists the people who misuse their belief for political purposes? It should not be hard to discern the right answer if one really wants to know. You can awaken the one who is asleep but it is not a good idea to try to awaken those who pretend they are sleeping. For the one who really wants to know who radicals are, it is obvious that the radical is the one who has taken his belief seriously and wants to obey and practice every bit of it. In other words those who are bound to their belief and accept all parts of it are true followers. On the other hand, somebody who accepts a part of a belief and rejects other parts can't really be called a true follower. When Bin Ladan is called radical, it makes me confused. Am I supposed to think that Bin Laden did not know Islam well? I wonder why he did not go to learn from a secular Muslim to be able to interpret Islamic rules in the proper way. Why aren't "radicals" persuaded by secular Muslims to forget about jihad, shave their beards, and have a happy life? Come to think about it, where are the secular Muslims who are trying to teach "radicals" that they have misunderstood Islam? Can they really support their ideas with the Koran and Sunnah?

Those radicals, fanatics, extremists—or whatever other terms are used for true Muslims—at least know Arabic many times better than so-called secular Muslims. For example, two of them, Sayed Qutb and Mustafa Azam, were hafizun—people who had memorized the entire Koran—before they were ten years old! If you check the citations used by the "radical" Muslim Abd al-Salam Faraj in his book Jihad: the Absent Obligation, you will see that he read at least 30,000 pages of writings uniformly accepted by Muslim scholars—both Sunni and Shia—as authoritative to produce his book. Faraj, you'll recall, was the inspiration for the Muslim Brothers who assassinated Sadat. Faraj's book shows the mindset of a famous jihadi. Ignoring jihadists' mindset and true beliefs leads a terrorism analyst in the wrong direction. The main argument is not why the authors call terrorists "radicals" because of their violent acts. The problem is when they call Islam "the religion of peace" that has nothing to do with jihad. Their assertion leads to the conclusion that there is something wrong with the so-called radicals' interpretation of Islamic sources. This is simply not true. If Islam is peaceful but jihadists are violent, logic would demand the conclusion that jihadists follow a belief other than Islam. Western academics, however, try to claim that Islam is peaceful but suggest jihadists have somehow misunderstood it, that is, they have come to a violent interpretation of something that is really peaceful. Because nobody doubts that jihadists are violent, we will focus on analyzing Islamic sources to see if Islam really has something to do with jihad and violence or not.

Before we begin to analyze Islamic sources I want to add a quick caveat about some of the arguments advanced by Muslim apologists. To a person like me who has been trained as a Muslim jurist, some of their arguments are as crazy as saying the West should not relate nuclear weapon to Islam because the word "nuclear" does not appear in the Koran. This example is a bit of hyperbole, but some of their arguments really do seem that crazy. Obviously, the real question is not whether the Koran names a particular weapon, but whether the Koran teaches Muslims to kill infidels. The point is, interpreting Islamic rules is not an easy job that everybody can do. One has to know Islamic sources well and also have been trained in the proper modes of reasoning to correctly elicit Islamic rules from the sources.

Graham Alison, a security expert, says,

> Osama bin Laden succeeded in getting a Saudi cleric to give him a fatwa which said that the use of nuclear weapons to accomplish this objective [killing infidels] would be legitimate in terms of Shari'ah law as interpreted by this particular Muslim cleric (Alison, 2004).

The way Graham Alison phrases this quotation suggests to the reader the Saudi cleric's fatwa is based on an incorrect interpretation. Using the term "particular" for the Saudi cleric creates a negative implication about the credibility of the issued fatwa. As previously noted, this is the way that security experts try to cover up the relation between jihadists and Islam. They even make the mistake of calling jihadists "crusaders." But maybe this is not a mistake, maybe the real purpose is to sow confusion by connecting jihadists' ideas to non-Islamic beliefs (Hacker, 1976).

Daniel (Ghasem) Akbari

Countries that Support Terrorism in the United States

There are numerous known and unknown Islamic organizations that directly or indirectly support Jihadi terrorist attacks against infidels. After the 9/11 attack, almost everybody knows that Al-Qaeda is one of the most active jihadi organizations, but there are also many other organizations—both foreign and domestic—that support jihadists. Because their support is done in the name of religion and is indirect, even mentioning the names of these organizations is not wise. Westerners just want to hear that the only supporters of terrorism are the regimes that have problems with the United States. Although it is certain that hostile foreign regimes do support terrorism, it is also true that some Islamic countries that are so-called allies of the U.S. are behind the majority of jihadi attacks.

There is no doubt that the Iranian Islamic government—a hostile foreign regime—is the biggest supporter of Hezbollah and Hamas. But Iran has a strategic plan which does not yet contemplate actually carrying out terrorist attacks in Western countries. To date they have simply been establishing the networks and infrastructure that would be necessary to carry out attacks in the future. Nowadays most of the advisors shaping Iran's foreign policy are people who studied at Western universities. They are smart enough to pay a big price for a small benefit. They know that carrying out a terrorist attack would, at most, kill a few thousand people, but it would turn the nations of the world even more strongly against Iran than they are already over Iran's nuclear program. Iran's main goal is to make progress on their nuclear program with fewer problems from the world community. They will avoid any act that might unify the world's opinion against them unless it also brings a big benefit. When an Iranian was arrested recently for a plot to assassinate the Saudi ambassador to the United States, security experts who know Middle Eastern politics did not take this news seriously. They understood Iran's true goals and knew that this type of attack would never be supported by the Iranian regime. Killing an ambassador—who would be swiftly replaced—would carry no benefit for Iran. Western media and politicians tend to focus on Iran as the principal sponsor of Islamic jihad, but this is a delusion that prevents us from seeing how big the threat of jihad really is. It is true that almost all terrorist attacks in Israel carried out by Hamas and Hezbollah are sponsored by Iran. Also some attacks against U. S. interests overseas before the 1990s were carried out by Hezbollah supported by Iran, such as the 1983 Marine barracks bombing in Beirut. But nowadays, because of the desire to complete their nuclear program, the Iranian Islamic regime avoids being a part of terrorist acts against Western targets. Nonetheless it is certain that the Iranian Islamic regime is carefully preparing their jihad network for a possible future war. This includes putting an organization in place in the United States to carry out attacks. During the Cold War, the USSR did the same thing, carefully staging KGB teams with preselected targets, like the Federal Reserve payment centers. For the present time, the major foreign terrorist threat to the US originates from countries whose rulers are friends with the United States, but whose people are not. Domestically, through non-violent Islamic centers, faithful Muslims recruit passionate Muslim youth and prepare them for jihadi attacks in the U.S. and overseas. Mainstream Western media diverts American's attention from the real threats calling them "non-violent Islamic organizations," for temporary politically correct benefits, but ultimately this deception will bring severe negative consequences to this country.

I do not think it is a coincidence that Tunisians and Egyptians rose against their rulers after the U.S. rejected the Palestinians' request from the U.N to be recognized as a country. The Tunisians and Egyptians found their rulers to be friends with countries that are "enemies to Islam" because they oppose Palestinian statehood. For Americans to feel safe from Islamic countries whose rulers are U.S allies but whose people are not is a tremendous security mistake. The U.S. immigration issues visas more readily for the citizens of these countries. When they come to the U.S and try to establish Islamic institutions they avoid suspicion because of the delusion that they are citizens of countries that are friends with the United States. The citizens of those so called secular Islamic countries count themselves as a part of "Umma", the Islamic nation. They believe in what their prophet Muhammad said that "if a Muslim hears his Muslim brother calling for help and does not help him, he is not a Muslim." This is why Tunisians and Egyptians rose against their rulers. They believed that their Palestinian brothers were calling for help but they did nothing. They found the cause of this failure in their rulers who were trusting and following Western leaders. Western countries assume that Muslims in free counties like the United States get fascinated with the sparkle of life—that is, having a good job and nice life—and do not try to be real followers of Islamic rules. This might be true if there were not so many so-called "peaceful, non-violent Islamic organizations" around to teach Muslims the truth about Islam.

Chapter Two

The Cost of Standing for Truth

The cost of telling the truth about Islam in Western countries is much higher than doing so in Islamic countries. If you analyze Islam truthfully—that is, you recognize that Islam is not a religion of peace—nobody in an Islamic country would even bother to oppose you. You won't be excommunicated from society or academia. The reason is that every single person who lives there would admit that you are not fabricating a heresy. They are familiar with Islamic rules enough to agree that fighting against non-Muslims is an integral part of the religion. But in Western countries, in particular the United States, if one claims that jihadi attacks are motivated by Islam, almost everybody will attack your idea by any available means. A vast majority of these Western critics do not know anything about Islam but they will try to hire a so-called "moderate" Muslim to attack your ideas about Islam. What is behind this advocacy is a mysterious phenomenon. If one can twist

Islamic rules to present Islam as a religion of peace, all media and pulpits will welcome you. Conversely, people who tell the truth that Islam is not peaceful and support their claim with tons of credible Islamic sources, all of a sudden, even the local radio station will refuse to give them an opportunity to speak. It is incredible how people have to self-censor themselves in democratic society even more than in Islamic countries when it comes to Islamic issues.

The danger of telling the truth about Islam in the United States is not a danger that threatens life; it damages one's status and career.

New Jihadists

If we count the September 11 attack as the start of a new generation of international terrorism against the United States, the Boston Marathon bombing was definitely the dawn of the new generation of domestic terrorism. This new generation of domestic terrorist are new Jihadists who do not need any foreign support. Passionate, smart youth who utilize whatever they learn from the United States education system against the country's own interest. They speak English fluently without any accent. They dress like Westerners. They have girlfriends. In one word, they are American. What differentiates these new Jihadists from ordinary American kids is that, despite their appearance, their hearts belong to their Islamic roots. By "roots" I mean the connection that links them to Islam, not necessarily their ethnicity or ties to any particular country of origin. For example, Tamerlan Tsarnaev—an ethnic Chechen—followed a Lebanese sheik for the Islamic ideas that inspired the Boston bombing. The same can be said about Naser Abdo, a white American kid in the U.S. Army who became a Muslim and plotted a copy-cat attack at Fort Hood, following Nidal Hassan, the Fort Hood terrorist.

It is hard for Muslims to put the United States' values above Islam's interest. Even though they take an oath to fight against their own countries in case of a war between the United States and their own homeland, they don't take that oath seriously. Islam would actually command them to make taqiyya in these situations. An example of this situation is the Fort hood shooting in which the Army psychiatrist unleashed fire on his fellow soldiers. This attack is evidence that proves Islamic belief for Muslims is more important than being American. Nadal Malik Hasan, the Fort hood army psychiatrist, was born in the United States. He was never by any definition a "radical" Muslim. But in the conflict between Islam and the United States interest, he opened fire and killed 13 Americans shouting Allah-O-Akbar (Allah is greater).

It is extremely difficult to recognize the traits of those who engage in terroristic attacks. So far, terrorists from all social classes have launched attacks in the United States citizens. From rich to poor, young and middle age, and "radical" to "moderate", this country has suffered a lot of pains. The only thing that is common among the majority of those attacks is Islam. In the future the majority of jihadi attacks would be accomplished by young male moderate Muslims who have studied at the United States' universities and are capable of planning, perpetrating, and targeting American citizens independently, without help from outside the U.S borders. In the past, when terrorists were dependent for help on known jihadi organizations outside the United States, it was easier for Homeland Security to track them down. But nowadays, every self-trained person can explode a bomb anywhere they want, so discovering the terroristic act in advance is tremendously difficult. There will be another difference between future jihadi attacks and past attacks that involved suicide. The young moderate Muslims are not interested in suicide attacks. Unlike "radicals," they prefer to stay alive to launch more attacks. For that purpose they tend to come up with smart ideas to accomplish the mission without getting killed.

The new generation of jihadists is afraid of assimilating into the U.S culture. Material prosperity is not the first priority in life for these young, moderate jihadis. They also are not necessarily motivated to wage jihad in order to go to heaven and sleep with seventy two virgins. Their real motivation is honor. They want to get rid of the humiliation the Muslim Umma—and their own families—have felt for not being above non-Muslims. Islam demands that Muslims be superior to non-Muslims at all times and in all things, because Islam is superior to unbelief and polytheism. We'll look at this requirement in more depth in a later chapter. These new Jihadists want to fulfill their parents' dream, which is doing something for the purpose of giving glory to Islam. "In order to understand the phenomenon of terrorism, scholars must look beyond the act itself and focus on the motivations behind it" (Pedahzur, 2005). Muslim parents, peers, and mosques are the ones that encourage these youth to send fear into non-Muslims' hearts, so when in the future Muslims want to demand their right to live under Islamic rules, non-Muslims will not resist.

Chapter Three

Important Islamic Sources

Even though it would be true to say that after the September 11 attacks, almost all Americans have heard of Islam, it is also true that the majority of Americans do not know what Islam really teaches. To know Islam, it is crucial to know Sharia. Sharia is something more than just the Koran. Sharia is the Koran, hadith, and the teachings of Muslim scholars followed by the recognized Islamic legal schools. Next to the Koran, the hadith is the second most authoritative source in Islam. The hadith is the purported sayings, deeds, and silences of Muhammad. Since Muhammad is the osvat-el-hassana—the perfect example of how to practice Islam, the hadith helps Muslims to understand the Koran. The hadith have been compiled by Muslim scholars from the sayings narrated by Mohammad's trusted companions. Some of those trusted companions include Mohammad's wives, his fathers-in-law, his son-in-law, and others. Some of them, like Abu-Backr (his father-in-law), Omar (another father-in-law), and Ali Ibn Abee Talib (His cousin and his son-in law) became caliph (successor) after Mohammad died. Ayesha (one of Mohammad's wives) who was trusted and close to Mohammad is another narrator of the recorded hadith.

Based on these narrations which are recorded in collections called "Sohah"—meaning they are considered to be the most authentic—Muslim scholars are able to explain the Koran. Without hadith it is impossible to understand the Koran. Sohah is the plural form of "sahih" and there are six hadith collections that are considered to make up the sohah. Each collection individually is called "sahih." So by knowing the Koran, hadith, and the history of Islam, famous Muslim scholars have made Sharia. Sharia is a collection of Islamic rules that govern every aspect of a Muslim's life, from the moment that a Muslim kid is born until the grave. When a Muslim child is born, somebody prays into his/her ears to make him/her Muslim. Beginning from that time, the baby is under Sharia until it dies. To understand the process of inferring Sharia rules from the Koran and hadith, an example might be helpful. Let's take the example of rules for female dress. The Hijab is mandatory for Muslim women. This is a Sharia rule. One might ask for evidence that supports it. Going step by step, the first and most authoritative source must always be the Koran. In Koran, Sura 33:59 says:

> O prophet! Say to your wives and your daughters and the women of the believers to put outer wrapper upon them. This will be more proper, that they may be known {from non-Muslim women and slaves} and thus they will not be given trouble; And Allah is forgiving, merciful.

The second source that Muslim scholars draw from is the hadith. For example:

> Ali bin Abi Talhah reported Ibn Abbas (trusted hadith narrators) said that Allah has commanded the believing

women, when they went out of their houses for some need, to cover their faces from above their heads with the outer wrapper leaving only one eye showing.

A number of ahadith—plural for hadith—may be offered to support a particular point of Sharia. Muslim scholars assess the validity of each hadith and its consistency with other important sources. They also employ rules for harmonizing conflicts among different authoritative sources called "usul-al-fiqh." Following this process, Muslims scholars come to a consensus agreement—ijma—that a particular thing is required by Sharia. The consensus among Muslim scholars (ijma) gives credibility to the Sharia rule throughout all of the Umma.

High ranking Muslim scholars are qualified to abandon some Islamic rules temporarily for a bigger Islamic purpose. They may also give authority to ordinary Muslims to abandon a rule of Sharia by announcing a fatwa. A fatwa is just a decree issued by high-ranking Muslim scholars for contemporary issues that might temporarily ban something which is allowed in Islam, or allow something which is taboo in Islam, all for the benefit of Islam. Unlike some Koranic verses that are ambiguous, the verses about jihad are clear and without any ambiguity and Muslim scholars have consensus that jihad is physical action against non-Muslims.

Sharia has comprehensive rules for people's interactions. Even though the majority of Sharia rules like different, unequal rights for men and women or chopping a thief's hands are against Human Rights Conventions, but they satisfy Islamic community needs. Unequal rights for men and women or cutting thieves' hands are supported by the Koran. From the custody of children to the color of a Muslim's dress, Sharia has a rule that must be followed by all Muslims. Some Islamic counties like Iran, Afghanistan, and Saudi Arabia enforce Sharia, but some others like Turkey have a secular system. In Islamic countries with Sharia law systems, the government is in charge for enforcing Islamic rules, but in counties like Turkey, even though the official legal system is not Sharia law, people do follow Sharia and enforce it informally within their families.

Establishing Sharia law throughout the entire world is the most important goal in Islam. The Koran in Sura 5:47-48 explains that everybody has to be judged by the rules of Allah (Sharia). Al-Misri, in his famous book, "The Reliance of the Traveller" says, "Islam is the final religion that Allah will never abrogate until the last day." He quotes 5:3 from the Koran that states: "Today I have perfected your religion for you and completed my favor upon you, and I am pleased that your religion is Islam." To achieve the goal of establishing Allah's rules throughout the world, different Muslims use different methods. Some, who are not attached to the material and the world carry out the exact order of the Koran and wage jihad. Others, who want to be Muslim and also enjoy their lives, use Dawa—Calling non-Muslims to Islam—to try to grow the number of Muslims, and also misuse the guaranteed freedom that has been given to American citizens by the constitution. They use their freedom to spread sedition, the demand that the U.S. government be overthrown and Sharia put in its place. To establish Sharia, the first step is to convince Americans that Sharia only applies to Muslims. Then, in the next step, since Islam wants to rule the whole world, the advocators of Sharia try to make it the law for the whole country.

Shia and Sunni

Since Mohammad started his mission as a prophet, the first people who believed in him and followed him were his first wife, Khadeeja, and his young cousin, Ali Ibn Abeetalib. Abeetalib (Mohammad's uncle and Ali's father) had many children and could not feed them all. So Mohammad adopted Ali who was a young kid to raise him and make his uncle's load lighter. The first years of Mohammad's mission in Mecca were very difficult for him and his followers. Ali, as one of Mohammad's most zealous followers, jeopardized his life to save Mohammad on many occasions. When the people of Mecca decided to kill Mohammad, Ali slept in Mohammad's bed to mislead the attackers and give Mohammad the opportunity to escape from Mecca. In the Battle of Uhud—where the Muslims were defeated—Ali was one of Mohammad's bodyguards and saved Mohammad's life.

Ali married Mohammad's daughter, Fatima, and this marriage drew him even closer to Muhammad. But it does not mean that Mohammad's other companions, like Abu Bakr and Omar, were not trusted by Mohammad. Both Abu Bakr and Omar were Mohammad's fathers-in-law. Ayesha (Abu Bakr's daughter) and Hafsa (Omar's daughter) were Mohammad's wives until he died.

After Mohammad's death, Muslims accepted Abu Bakr as Mohammad's successor (the first caliph). This made Ali and two other famous Muslim companions—Talhe and Zobeir—angry. They did not want to accept Abu Bakr as the caliph. Omar, on the other hand, accepted Abu-Bakr as Mohammad's successor and forced Ali, Talhe, and Zobeir to do so and they did. Shia Muslims believe that Mohammad chose Ali to be his successor. But Sunni Muslims believe differently. Even though Sunnis respect Ali as the fourth Caliph and one of Mohammad's companions, they are upset with Shia Muslims' insistence on Ali's right as Mohammad' real successor. Mohammad never appointed his successor. He did not want to split Islam at the beginning; however, it happened after his death. Abu Bakr was the head of a big tribe and had many supporters. On the other hand, Ali was alone and nobody supported his bid to be caliph.

Ali did eventually become caliph. Not the first one but the fourth one. Some Sunni Muslims accuse Ali for the assassination of the third caliph, Osman, an accusation that Shia Muslims reject. Ali got assassinated by a group of Muslims who did not believe in paying tax to the caliph. Ali's sons could not become caliph because of opposition by the Muslims who would become known as Sunnis. Ali's oldest son, Hasan, gave up his claim to be claiph and compromised with a Meccan named Moaweea, who became the fifth caliph. Ali's youngest son, Hossain, gathered a small group and rose against Moaweea's son Yazid, who became the sixth caliph. Hossain and his followers got killed in the city of Karbala, a city in Iraq. The caliph's army beheaded Hossain and took his family captive. They were forced to march from Karbala to Damascus.

Shia Muslims mourn for Hossain every year for almost forty days. Hossain is the symbol of martyrdom for Shia Muslims. They believe that Hossain sought martyrdom voluntarily. Koran does not command suicide attacks. Koran commands jihad, and promises that a Muslim who is slain while killing non-Muslims will be rewarded with paradise. Dying in jihad is the only way to be certain of going to heaven in Islam. For Shia Muslims, however, suicide attacks have a special significance, because of the martyrdom of Hossain. Shia Muslims have used suicide attacks for 1400 years when they are weaker than their enemies. Iran, Iraq, and Bahrain are Shia-dominated countries, but some counties like Lebanon also have significant Shia populations. Mourning for Hossain—considered by Shia Muslims as the third Imam—is the central part of Shia belief. Shia leaders misuse the passion that their people have for the third Imam to encourage them to seek martyrdom whenever the leaders feel it is necessary. Shia leaders (Mullas) warn their people that if they forget the idea of "seeking martyrdom" they will be humiliated before their enemies. They say: "A nation that has the culture of martyrdom never suffers humiliation." "Humiliation" in Islam is defined as anything that makes a Muslim to become weaker than non-Muslims. Based on this interpretation of "humiliation," Shia Muslims consider the idea of seeking martyrdom as a way of escaping the psychological pressure of failing to accomplish anything—for example developing their national economy and industry—in which non-Muslims have been more successful. Their is even a special term in Arabic—remember, not all Shia are Farsi-speaking Persians—for the idea of seeking martyrdom: "esteshad."

The majority of Shia Muslims believe in twelve Imams. The "Twelfth Imam" is known as "Mahdee"—the one Shias believe to be "The savior of the world." Both Sunnis and Shias believe in the Mahdee, but Sunnis do not believe him to be the Twelfth Imam. It is a part of Shia belief that Allah has hidden Mahdee and he will be returned when the world is full of injustice. Mahdee is believed to be the real leader of the Islamic nation. Since in the absence of Mahdee, Shia Muslims need a leader, the most knowledgeable Shia scholar who represents the Mahdee leads the Shia nation. In Iran, for instance, Khamanei has occupied that position. Even though some Iranians do not accept him as the most knowledgeable scholar, those who believe he is qualified enough to represent Mahdee helped him to become the leader of the Shia nation. Therefore the Iranian Supreme leader, Khamenei, is in the position to organize all the available resources to extend Shia Muslims power in the Islamic world.

Unlike Sunni Muslims, Shias do not respect Sunni caliphs. Shia rejects almost all the hadith narrated by those companions of Mohammad who are respected by Sunni Muslims. Mohammad's wife, Ayesha, and Omar, the second caliph, are the companions that Shia Muslims most criticize. Because Shia Muslims reject most of the ahadith that are considered authentic (Sahih), it is easy to understand why they are criticized for having an incomplete understanding of Islam. Sunni people count Shia as a heresy. Some Sunni extremist even call Shias, infidels. This is why we see so much violence between Sunni and Shia Muslims, for example in Syria, Iraq, and Lebanon as this book is being written.

Chapter Four

Islam and Jihad

Meccan and Medinan verses

The most important Islamic source trusted by all Muslims is the Koran. In this book we discuss the Koranic issues related to jihad; but to give you a better understanding of the relation between Islam and jihad, we need to explain the tenets and principles that come from all the authoritative sources and make up the whole of Islam just as any good Islamic scholar would. The Koran has 114 chapters (Suras). Some of those Suras were revealed to Mohammad in Mecca and some others in Medina. When non-experts read the Koran, they will find many contradictions. Does the Koran have contradictions about how Muslims should treat non-Muslims? Definitely not! So why does a non-expert who reads the Koran get that misunderstanding? The trick is to understand a concept called "abrogation" (al-nasikh wa al-mansukh). To abrogate simply means to cancel something. In Islam, Koranic verses can be abrogated either explicitly or impliedly. Abrogation works very simply in the Koran—the verses that were revealed later in time cancel or "abrogate" earlier verses if the later verses contradict the earlier ones. Based on Islamic history, Meccan verses—the verses revealed while Mohammad was in Mecca, before moving to Medina—precede Medinan verses—the verses revealed to Mohammad in Medina. One might ask, "What are the differences between Meccan verses Medinan verses other than just some are earlier in time? This is a significant question that needs to be answered properly and carefully to avoid any confusion and misunderstanding. When Mohammad was in Mecca, he didn't have power. He was a peaceful preacher. Even though his wife Khadija was wealthy, that wealth did not give Mohammad power, however it did help him to start his mission. So far we have a peaceful man who preached tolerance with non-Muslims. He didn't force his god, Allah, on non-Muslims. In the Meccan verses, Mohammad said non-Muslims had their god and he had his god. He absolutely refused to worship the many gods of the Meccans, but he did not, at that time, force them to worship Allah. When Mohammad immigrated to Medina and gathered an army, he changed his attitude toward non-Muslims. Medinan verses are the result of Mohammad being not only a prophet, but also the head of an army whose purpose, ultimately, became spreading Islam throughout the entire world. In Medinan verses, which abrogate those nice Meccan verses about non-Muslims, Mohammad ordered his followers to kill those who disbelieve in Allah as god and Mohammed as the prophet. Now you know enough about Islam to solve the mystery of the perceived contradictions in the Koran. There is no contradiction, just abrogation. An army commander might order his troops to start shooting. When the soldiers are about to shoot, the commander orders them not to do so. Doesn't the latter order cancel the former one? Of course, and this is just what we mean by abrogation in the Koran.

Now that we have basic knowledge about the Meccan and Medinan verses, we can analyze the very last chapter (sura) that was revealed to Mohammad in Medina; it is Sura 9. The name of the Sura (chapter) is Bera'a or Taoba. Bera'a means: Muslims are not bound to any obligation in the case of dealing with non-Muslims any more. Unlike all other 113 Suras, Sura 9 does not start with the name of Allah as a compassionate and merciful god. Allah is angry with non-Muslims in this Sura which is the last Sura ever revealed, based on Al-Bukhari whose hadith collection is the second most important Islamic source after the Koran. We can logically conclude that this chapter is that last intention of Mohammad about dealing with infidels (non-Muslims).

"The Verse of the Sword"

The Koran uses different terms for non-Muslims. Because our focus is jihadi acts in the United States against American citizens, who are perceived by jihadists as "Christians," we will use the term that the Koran applies to Christian and Jews. The term is "Ahl-ul-kitab" which means: the people of the scripture. Other terms like Kafir (unbeliever) or Moshrik (polytheist)—both of which are considered to be infidels—also apply to Christians and Jews. In Sura 5 verse 72 and Sura 9 verse 30, for instance, the Koran applies both the Kafir and Moshrik terms to Christians who are cursed by Allah. From now on in this book, when we see any of these terms—Ahl-ul-kitab, Kafir, or Moshrik—in a verse from Koran, remember they all apply to non-Muslim American citizens. The reason why we are getting into specific details is because Muslim spokesmen try to persuade Americans that the Koran excludes Christians from being attacked. But the obvious question then is what do Muslim spokesmen say about the Koranic commands for killing Chinese? Does Koran command Muslims to kill Chinese, because they are neither Muslims nor Christians? With regard to Christians, Sura 9:29 orders Muslims to give them three choices: 1) continue to fight against Muslims, and the Muslims will continue to make jihad until they kill all who resist, 2) become Muslims and the Muslims will stop fighting them, or 3) surrender to the political control of Islam and pay the Jizya. They can stay in their Christian religion but they become second-class citizens in Muslim society. Jihadists, at least their leaders, know all these details about their own faith. So they are not misinterpreting the Koran's definition that applies the terms Moshrek, Kafir, or people of scripture to non-Muslim American citizens. All the verses in the Koran and all the Sharia rules serve just one purpose and that is to make Allah's religion (Islam) supreme (Sura 8:39). So if American citizens "feel themselves subdued" and pay the Jizya (a special tax that people of the scripture have to pay to be allowed to practice their religion, even though they do not have the right to repair their worship places or share their faith) the way that Sharia law provides, they would not get killed. To establish Allah's religion firm in the whole world, the Koran orders Muslims to make jihad by sacrificing their lives and property (Sura 9:20).

Does Jihad really matter in Islam?

Many great Muslim scholars who are expert in explaining the Koran (Mofassereen ul-Koran) have called the fifth verse of Sura 9 of the Koran "the verse of the sword". This verse has abrogated (revoked or canceled) 114 verses out of 54 Suras. Ibn Kathir who is the author of one of the most well-known Mofassereen (those who have explained the Koran) said:

> Verily it [sura 9:5] abrogated every treaty, contract and terms between the Prophet and anyone from the Mushrikun (non-Muslims). Al-Awfi reported Ibn Abbas (two of the hadith narrators) to have said about this verse: *"No treaty or covenant was left for anyone from the Mushrikun after Surah 9:5 (Baraa or at-Tawbah) was revealed.*

Sura 9:5 expressly states: "Then kill the Muskhrikun (Non-Muslims) wherever you find them." Another Sura—2:216 says "Fighting is prescribed for you" and cancels all the verses that contradict it. Therefore any verse of the Koran that suggests tolerating non-Muslims is not valid since Sura 9:5 was revealed. Another Muslim scholar called Al-Hussain ibn Fadhl said this about abrogated verses:

> The verse of the sword abrogated every verse of the Quraan in which turning away from the harm of the enemies and being patient with them is mentioned. It is strange of the one, who (still) uses abrogated verses as evidences to abandon fighting and Jihaad (Faraj,).

The Koran gives Muslims instruction for fighting by saying: "So when you meet those who disbelieve [Islam] smite their necks (Sura 47:4)." Some Muslims who have translated the Koran to English have added words such as (in fighting or on the battlefield) after the words "when you meet them, but these extra words are not present in the original Arabic and are probably added just to mislead Westerners. The extra words added to Sura 47:4 also contradict the Sword Verse's explicit command to "kill them wherever you find them." The word "wherever" speaks for itself and does not need any translation. To explain the word wherever and the application of it, Ibn Kathir says:

> Then fight the Mushrikin wherever you find them and capture them, executing some and keeping some as prisoners, and besiege them, and lie in wait for them in each and every ambush, do not wait until you find them. Rather, seek and besiege them in their areas and forts, gather intelligence about them in the various roads and fairways so that what is made wide looks ever smaller to them. This way, they will have no choice, but to die or embrace Islam.

Al Bukhari's hadith collection, the second most important Islamic source after the Koran, has recorded a hadith from one of Mohammad's companions which states, "A man came to Allah's Messenger and said: Guide me to such a deed as equals Jihad in reward. He replied: I do not find such a deed." (Sahih-al-Bukhari)." Another hadith recorded in Sahih Abu Dawood says: "Jihad will continue until the Day of Judgment." This hadith disproves those who claim that jihad only belonged to Muhammad's era. There are tons of verses in the Koran that give a very high value to jihad. Muslim spokesmen frequently try to diminish the importance of fighting non-Muslims by claiming that there is a "greater jihad"—a more important jihad in Islam—that simply means fighting sin in an individual's life. But there is no such term as "greater jihad" in the Arabic of any authentic Islamic sources. In many places in the Koran, it has been said expressly that jihad means physical attack. To make it clear, Sura 8:60 orders Muslims to make their horses ready to attack, which would be nonsense to interpret as using horses to attack sin in a person's heart. The targets of jihad have always been identified in the Koran as infidels, not even once as the hearts of the Muslims. There is just one hadith that has become the source of the Muslim spokesmen's claim, but it is not consistent with the Koran. In the conflict between a hadith and a verse in the Koran, the hadith that contradicts the Koran must be rejected, not the Koranic verse, or, in the case of jihad, dozens of Koranic verses.

Another tactic that Muslim spokesmen use to make Islam seem harmless is the so called "Five Pillars." The "Five Pillars" are the five religious practices that were revealed to Mohammed while he was in Mecca (Ali Dashti, 1985). They do not include jihad as an important pillar of Islam. Muslim spokesmen highlight a hadith called the "Gabriel Hadith" as evidence for the Five Pillars. This hadith does not classify Islamic practices the way Muslim scholars do. It just mentions some of Islamic duties and excludes many others that are at least equally important. But those spokesmen make a big deal out of it to depreciate the importance of jihad, which is the most important duty paced on Muslims' shoulders according to the Koran and other important Islamic sources.

The living example of the importance of physical jihad are the lands occupied by Muslims from Indonesia to Morocco. Even a small knowledge of Islamic history proves that all those Islamic countries have been conquered by jihad, which was obviously physical attacks against non-Muslims. Sura 9:5 states ". . . slay infidels wherever you find them, take them captives, besiege them, and lie in wait for them . . ." Another verse from the same Sura, 9:55, provides: "Do not let their (infidels) children and property excite your admiration; Allah only wishes to torture them by that in this world and torture their souls when they die, [because] they are infidels." The exact verse has been repeated in the same Sura in verse 85 as well. We are not taking verses out of context as some might claim. My analysis of Islamic issues in this book follows the same methodology that all Muslims scholars have employe throughout Islamic history. This book avoids claiming anything that the authentic Islamic sources do not support. Sura 33:61 orders Muslims to "seize the cursed people (i.e. infidels) wherever found and kill them in a horrible way." Those so called radicals or jihadists read the Koran not every day but every moment. If they are not reading they are listening. So criticizing them for misunderstanding the Koran is not wise if we truly want to understand their motivation for attacking American citizens. In Sura 33:62, the Koran expressly rejects the idea that those rules are only for 1400 years ago. It says: "That was the Way of Allah in the case of those who passed away of old: and you will not find any change in the Way of Allah." Muslims know that the Koranic verses are forever and never go out of date. Remember, we are analyzing Islam. We are not trying to say whose idea is better or closer to the Universal Declaration of Human Rights or is a better way to live in peace. We are analyzing to see whose actions and behavior are more Islamic. Islam, in many ways, rejects Westerners' ideas about life, political systems and women's rights. Equal rights for women and men is, undeniably, considered to be right by Westerners, but equal rights for the sexes is against the Koran. The West is encouraging Afghans to enact rules that give equal rights to women. This encouragement is the result of the lack of knowledge about Islam. If one just opens the Koran to Sura 4:34, they will see that equality is against the Koran. All the above discussion is to make it clear that the Jihadists' interpretation of Islamic sources is the closest to what Mohammad meant and did.

Taqiyya

To protect Islam and make it successful, Muslims are allowed to hide their faith and also lie to deceive non-Muslims. For example, Koran teaches that non-Muslims are unclean and should not be allowed to enter a mosque. But moderate Muslims, trying to make Islam seem less threatening, might let non-Muslims in their mosque. They might even eat pork with them to be able to get established in the United States. Many prominent Muslim leaders in the United States, while they agree with the ultimate goal that Islam must be supreme, disagree with radicals in the method of attaining that supremacy. Most of these moderate leaders have lived in the United States long enough to know that they are not powerful enough to force Americans to accept the supremacy of Islam at this point. It is noteworthy to mention an event from Islamic history where Taqiyya was used.

Abu Ja'far—known to Muslim scholars as al-Tabari—one of the most important Muslim historians says when the Meccans suffered disaster at Badr—Mohammed's first major attack on the Meccans' caravans—Mohammad sent two people to Medina to take the good news of the victory Allah granted to him and the killing of a number of polytheists. Ka'b Bin Ashraf was a man from the Tayyi tribe. His mother was a Jewish woman from the Bani Natheer clan. When Ka'b heard the news he said: If truly Mohammad has killed those known warriors people are talking about, then the belly of the earth would be a better place for us than the surface of it. He also composed some poems about Muslims. According to Ibn Homayd, the Prophet said: "who will get rid of Ibn Ashraf for me?" Muhammad Bin Maslameh—one of the Muslims said: "O Messenger of Allah, I will kill him." "Then do it!" The prophet said, "if you can." Bin Maslameh could not eat or drink for three days after that day. The Prophet heard of that and asked him why he had stopped eating and drinking. Bin Maslameh said: "O Messenger of Allah, I have promised something and I don't know whether I can fulfill it." "All you need to do is to give it a try," the Prophet replied. "O Messenger of Allah," he said, "we will have to lie." "Say whatever you need to," the prophet replied. "You are forgiven for that." Then Muhammad Bin Maslameh, enlisted the help of Silkan bin Salamah, the foster brother of Ka'b bin Ashraf, and some other Muslims. They got prepared to go and kill Ka'b bin Ashraf (the Poet who was the target).

It was Ka'b's wedding night and he was sleeping on the roof of his house along with his bride, because it was Spring time (Rabie-ol Awwal). Ka'b's foster brother called him and asked him to come to the door. The bride said; "Don't go! It is night time and we don't know what would happen." "He is my brother. We grew up together, so don't worry" Ka'b replied. When Ka'b got to the door, his foster brother told him that "he was right about Mohammad the prophet." He continued "the arrival of Mohammad the Prophet brought misery to us and we have nothing to eat. Our families are starving. Would you lend us some food?" Ka'b said: "I warned you about that." Ka'b agreed to give him food. The foster brother said: "I have some friends with me who are in the same situation so treat them generously, too." He continued: "they have brought swords to give you as pawn." He didn't want to make his brother suspicious when other attackers approached him. Ka'b agreed so. They all came out of the ambush and approached him. Ka'b's foster brother got close to him and said: "your hair smells good." Then he grabbed Ka'b's hair and restrained him as the others attacked and killed him (Tareekh-al-Tabaree).

The story teaches three principles about Taqiyya. First, to accomplish a mission that benefits Islam, you are allowed to lie.

The second principle is that Silkan bin Salemah put Islam above his relationship with his brother and plotted against him. The last principle is that Silkan bin Salemah even said bad things about Prophet Muhammad in order to carry out the mission. This historical event has been recorded in at least three famous Islamic sources trusted by all Islamic schools including: Syrat-al-Nabee by Ibn Ishak, Tareekh-al-Tabaree by Abu Ja'far, and Saheeh-al-Bukhari.

"The Absent Obligation"

In his book, <u>The Absent Obligation</u>, Abdus Salam Faraj thoroughly discusses Jihad as an important duty as significant as the Islamic religion itself. Faraj supports his claim about Jihad with Islamic sources that are so widely accepted that no Muslim could argue its credibility. Most of them are verses from the Koran. To explain those verses, he uses authentic hadiths from the Sohah hadith collections. He analyzes Jihad in the same way as Ibn Taymeya, who is considered one of the most knowledgeable Islamic scholars of all time. Understanding Faraj's ideas is crucial, because it helps us to find out what is going on in the mind of the Jihadi leaders whose arguments persuade young Muslims to stand for Islam and attack non-Muslims. In his famous book, <u>The Absent Obligation</u>, Faraj states: "A nation does not abandon Jihad in the way of Allah, except that it is humiliated." He quotes this idea from Sunan Abu Dawood, which is one of the important Sohah (authentic) hadith collections. Faraj's book is a message from one of the Jihadi leaders in Egypt. He quotes from the Koran to make the ultimate goal of Islam clear. For example, Sura 8:39 states: "And fight them until there is no more fitnah (worshiping anything other than Allah) and the religion is all for Allah."

To know Faraj better, here is some information about him:

Mohammad 'Abdus Salaam Faraj was born in 1952 at al-Baheerahad-Dalanjaat, in Egypt. By profession he was an electrical engineer at Cairo University. It is said that he was the Ameer of *Tandheem al-Jihaad* since 1979 and was responsible for bringing Khaalid al-Islaambouli into its fold, in 1980. This era was when the legions of the evil leaders of Egypt were carrying out their brutal repression against the Islamic movement. This they did after making unprecedented and unconditional treaties with the illegal state of Israel and subsequently earning the animosity of the Muslims. Indeed through writings such as 'The Absent Obligation' the author of this book became a household name amongst the Islamic movement in Egypt, alongside those of Sayyid Qutb and Sheikh 'Umar Abdur Rahman. These names were characterized with one cause—standing up and calling for the truth of Islam—even at the cost of their own lives. Mohammed 'Abdus Salaam Faraj was sentenced to death and executed by hanging in the Baab al-Khalq prison in central Cairo on 15th April 1982 along with two other companions, by the Phaoronic regime under the leadership of Husni Mubaarak. May Allaah shower his mercy on Mohammed 'Abdus Salaam Faraj and those who were killed with him. One of his quoted sayings remains: *"Take the news to the Jews: The army of Muhammad has returned! We are on our way to Jerusalem."* The year prior to his execution saw the assassination of President Anwar Sadat by Khaalid al-Islaambouli, who is reported to have said: '*I have killed Pharaoh.*'

There are other verses repeated many times in the Koran that say even immigrating out of lands controlled by Islam to lands where non-Muslims are in control for the cause of Allah is counted as a type of Jihad. This immigration for the cause of Allah could serve the ultimate goal of Islam, which is to make the religion of Islam reign supreme (Sura 8:72, Sura 2:218). Sura 8:72 states: "Verily, those who believed, and emigrated and strove hard and fought with their property and their lives in the cause of Allah as well as those who gave (them) asylum and help,—these are (all) allies to one another." Here Allah praises those believers who left their homes and estates in Mecca to help Muhammad establish the religion of Islam in Medina, giving them the title of "Muhajirin," the Arabic word that means emigrants. They gave up their wealth and themselves in this cause. This verse solves the mystery of why some Muslims whose women wear Niqab (the cloth that covers all of their face except the eyes), have trouble finding a store to buy Hilal meat (meat that has been slaughtered in an Islamic way), and who hold themselves separate and do not even try to assimilate into the American community nevertheless try to get citizenship no matter how difficult it might be. Living in the United States is kind of a torture for these Muslims. So why do they insist on having their children born here in the United States? This is nonsense unless we relate it to a type of Jihad which is emmigrating for the cause of Allah. One might say that they immigrate to the United States just to have a better life, but there is nothing in the United States that they enjoy but the freedom to expand Islam. Their women stay at home from morning to evening just raising kids and do not do anything that might be counted as a better life from a Westerner's point of view. Their struggle to live in the Western communities is for the cause of Allah. They expect reward from Allah for whatever "hardship" they have endured because of emigration from Islamic lands to live in the United States.

CHAPTER FIVE

WHO IS A SHEIKH?

A Sheikh is a Muslim who has devoted his life to studying Islamic sources—the Koran, the hadith, Islamic history, and Sharia law—also called "Fiqh"—to lead the Muslim community and teach them how to live on the path of Islam. The high ranking Sheikhs have millions of followers and issue effective Fatwas. Fatwa is an Islamic order issued by a Sheikh to give an Islamic solution on any issue. There is no limit to the issues that a Fatwa can cover. They range from daily issues in the lives of Muslims all the way to major rulings on politics, international relations, and war. This title is often used in a sloppy manner to refer to anybody who is interested in Islamic matters without regard to whether they have the training and knowledge to actually qualify for the title.

In the modern day there are some Sheikhs who are young but they have started learning about Islam from childhood, raised by parents who are true followers of Islam. Some of these young Sheikhs have grown up in Western countries and speak English fluently. They normally move back to their home countries after graduation from university. When they move back, they start to gather followers around them and establish an Islamic organization. They design a website and use all they have learned from Western Universities for advertising and recruiting young Muslims from all around the world. This new generation of Sheikhs are totally different than the older generation who could not speak any Western language or even turn a computer on. Young Muslims who live in the West value this new generation of Sheikhs. The young Sheikhs know how to address emotional problems that Muslim emmigrants' children might encounter in their daily life in the West. What enables them to do so is that they have experienced the same lifestyle in the West and understand the mindset of these young Muslims. This rapport helps young Muslims in the West to find Islamic ideas fascinating and something they were looking for. In addition, the young Muslims' parents encourage their children to follow these Sheikhs.

The young Sheikhs' language and computer skills, plus being connected to established and well-funded Islamic organizations, enable them to improve their followers' Islamic knowledge with free Islamic resources. They can answer almost every question about Islam's idea on any aspect of life from politics and economics, to propaganda and public relations. Social networks like Facebook, Twitter, and YouTube are used by these new Islamic leaders to expand Islam and encourage young Muslims to wage jihad. One example of these Sheikhs is Feiz Mohammad, who is believed to have influenced the Boston Marathon Bomber, Tamerlan-Tsarnaev. Feiz Mohammed is a young Sheikh who, like Tsarnaev, is also a boxer. He used to live in Australia but he decided to move back home and now he lives in Lebanon. In Australia he was one of the founders and the head of the Global Islamic Youth Center. He is a Salafee Muslim Sheikh. Salafees and Wahabees are two Islamic sects of Islam whose interpretation of Islamic sources could be counted as the true version of Islam. Walking on the path of Mohammad and the Koran is their main concern. Followers of Salafee and Wahbee sects are known as "radicals" in the West. The reason that Westerners call him "radical" is that he calls Jews, "pigs" and encourages Muslims to kill them. He also calls Muslims to kill "Koffar," all those who do not believe in Islam. He just preaches Islam and calling him something more than a true Muslim is a mistake. Whatever he teaches is backed up by authentic Islamic sources.

Living Under a Non-Islamic System as a Muslim

Mohammad the prophet of Islam said to the non-Muslims of Mecca when he was there: "O people of Quraish, listen to me! By the One in whose hand is my soul, indeed I have come to you with slaughter." By saying "I have come to you with slaughter," the Messenger of Allah drew the straight path which has no debate or compromise with the leaders of kufr. Kufr literally means "to cover," as in covering up the truth. In common use, kufr means anything other than Islam. Based on all of the authentic Islamic sources, the establishment of the "Caliphate"—the Islamic state—is the fulfillment of the Koran's command. As Faraj states in his book "it is obligatory upon every Muslim to do his utmost to implement them." The verses that support the idea of an Islamic state are Sura 5:49: "You judge between them by what Allah has revealed" and Sura 5:44: "Whoever does not rule by what Allah has revealed (the Koranic rules), such {people} are disbelievers." Muslims who live under non-Islamic rulers are commanded by the Koran, the hadith, the example of Muhammad and Islamic history, and the Sharia law of how to practice Islam correctly to rise up against non-Muslim rulers and establish Sharia law in their land. The growing Islamic awareness in Tunisia, Egypt, and Libya—the so-called "Arab Spring"—is an example of trying to bring the abandoned rules of Islam back to life. Jihadists believe that fighting is the most effective way to establish the Islamic state and therefore in incumbent upon Muslims to fight. There is just one condition that must exist to consider a state to be an Islamic state. In accordance with all the authoritative sources of Islam, that condition is that the state is governed by Islamic law. To fulfilling the mentioned verses, Islamic leaders (Sheikhs) use all modern technologies and resources like the internet and media to teach young Muslims and motivate them for carrying out Jihadi missions.

Jihadi Attacks by Muslims Who Serve in non-Muslim Governments

Ibn Taymiyyah is one of the most important Islamic scholars. He lived in the 13th century in Syria. Nobody questions his incredible knowledge in all areas of Islamic matters. All his Fataawa (plural of Fatwa) and his books are clear. In other words, he said what he meant. Because it is almost impossible in the Islamic world to ignore him, some 'moderate" Muslims claim that he has been misunderstood by "radicals." Those so-called moderate Muslims do not bother to prove their assertion. Ibn Taymiyyah in one of his Fattawa—Al-Fataawa: 28/535—discusses how Muslims should react when they see other Muslims who serve non-Muslims in any way (Al-Fareethat ol-Qaeba). He said:

> Thus it becomes clear that the one who is with them and is a Muslim by origin is more evil than those who are disbelievers (at that time), because when the Muslim apostatizes from some of the Shari'ah, his case becomes worse than the one who has not entered into it yet. Even if the apostates understand, write or practice some aspects from the laws of Islam they are worse than those who have not entered into the fold of Islam and its laws. Accordingly the Muslims find that they harm the religion more than the others, and they criticize the laws of Islam. So obedience to Allah and His Messenger is greater than saving those who have apostatized from part of the religion and show hypocrisy in part, even if they display some connection with Islamic knowledge and religion.

Based on Ibn Taymmyah, Muslims who serve the U.S. military or other branches of government could be either targets to be killed because of their cooperation with infidels or become Jihadists and attack their fellows. Nidal Malik Hasan, the U.S. Army psychiatrist who allegedly opened fire and killed at least 13 American soldiers, is an example of how some Muslims come to the conviction that, as a Muslim, they should not serve infidels, in particular when there is war between Muslims and Non-Muslims. Ibn Taymiyyah also said: "None of those who behave as Muslims would voluntarily join them unless he is a hypocrite (zindiq) or a wicked sinner. He continues:

> Whoever has joined them, from the military leaders or others, then the ruling on him is the same as the ruling on them, and that is they have apostatized from the laws of Islam.

Ibn Taymiyyah gives a reason for why those Muslims who join non-Muslims against Muslims, even under compulsion, need to be killed. He said: "And the one they took out with them by force will be resurrected according to his intention. But we have to fight the whole army, because it is not possible (for us) to distinguish between the one who is forced and the one who is not" (Al-Fataawa: 28/535). These are not Ibn-Taymeyyah's ideas. He has just analyzed Islamic rules and issued a Fatwa. So it is wrong to believe that this is just one person's idea and has nothing to do with Islam. Some people just open the Koran and read. When they cannot find, for example, the U.S. Army explicitly mentioned, they might conclude that a great Muslim scholar like Ibn Taymeyyah is wrong. As we mentioned before, understanding Islamic sources to be able to give an Islamic ruling to issues Muslims face is not an easy job that everybody can do. It requires knowledge, training, and experience. This is why everybody—even the majority of Muslim scholars—are not qualified to issue Fatwas. Only a small percentage of all Muslims scholars, perhaps one out of a million, who have studied Islam for their whole lives are qualified to issue Fatwa. Most of those "moderate" Muslims have never bothered to read the Koran even one time, something that many Americans after September 11 have done.

Five Pillars and Jihad

Almost all the books written in English about Islam introduce Islam as a religion that has just five elements. They embrace one hadith called the "Gabriel Hadith" to justify this characterization of Islam. This characterization is wrong and incomplete for these reasons: First, this classification puts belief in Allah and Mohammad on the same level with other pillars like Hajj (pilgrimage to Mecca). One can be Muslim but might not be able to afford to travel for the Hajj. If a Muslim cannot afford to make pilgrimage to Mecca, he is still a Muslim; but a person is not a Muslim if he does not believe in Allah and Mohammad. Second, Jihad is not been mentioned in this characterization although it is the most important Islamic pillar based on a many authentic ahadith recorded in Sahih-al-Bukhari and other hadith collections. Third, in many places in the Koran "enjoining good and forbidding evil" is as important as prayer, but it has not been counted as one of the pillars. Basing the characterization of Islam on the "Gabriel Hadith"—a single hadith that clearly omits other important material from the Koran and other Islamic sources—is a mistake. Mohammad said things based on particular circumstances, so to understand his intent one has to know those circumstances, called the "asbab ol-nuzul" (causes of inspiration), as well as the Koran and other ahadith to combine them and make a decision for characterizing the elements of Islam. Ibn-Taymyyah, as one of the most important Islamic scholars, has mentioned many hadith in which Jihad is the peak of pillars.

Even though it is politically correct to stick to "Five Pillars" as the elements of Islam, this mistaken view has some liabilities and negative effects as well. Westerners might think that it is good to advocate the idea of "Five Pillars" so Muslims would not think that

Jihad is something obligatory for them to be Muslims. Supporting the idea of "Five Pillars" has a negative side effect for Westerners, specifically those who only speak English and do not have access to Arabic sources for information about Islam. The negative effect for Westerners who do not know Arabic is that they remain ignorant about what Islam really teaches. The majority of Muslims speak another language other than English, so the idea of "Five Pillars" does not affect them as much as it does English speakers. However, the idea of "Five Pillars" is a good tool in the hand of the Muslim who lives in the West to disprove those who say Jihadists wage Jihad for the sake of Islam. Imagine how hard would be the job of somebody who wants to stand for the truth and convince everybody who has been misled about the connection between jihad and Islam.

"Jihad Akbar"

The true Islamic meaning of the term Jihad has already been explained and illustrated. Now it's time for dealing with another term, which is related to Jihad. This term is *"Jihad Akbar."* Akbar means greater. Therefore Jihad Akbar means greater Jihad. Strangely, by and large everyone who has read a book about Jihad has encountered the term "greater Jihad." Many of the authors who write about Jihad have never read the Koran, but claim to know what the term "greater Jihad" means. Why? The term "greater Jihad" comes originally from a book called "Al Zohd Al Kabir" written by a person called Beihaqee. How do all those authors who mention the term "greater Jihad" claim to know the meaning of "greater Jihad" without even knowing the name or author of the book where the term comes from? Beihaqee, the author of Al Zohd Al Kabir records a hadtith ascribed to Mohammad in which the "greater jihad" is defined as "fighting against evil temptation." First of all, it should be noted that this hadith has been classified as a fake hadith by the majority of Islamic scholars throughout history, including Beihaqee himself.

Beihagee said this hadith was weak, meaning it was not trustworthy. Ibn Tamayya went farther, calling it "gharib," meaning it is "strange" or not authentic at all. The reason that most of those authors who write about Islam know this fake hadith but don't know the Koran as the most important source of Islam is that there is a planned propaganda to make this fake hadith an authentic source and hide the true teachings of the Koran itself.

In Islamic studies, there is an Islamic science called, Elm-ol-Hadith. Elm-ol-Hadith is a mix of logic and Islamic history. This Islamic science enables the Muslim scholar to distinguish fake ahadith from authentic ahadith. Even though the purpose of this book is not to teach Elm-ol-Hadith, explaining its principles would be beneficial. The first principle is no hadith should contradict the Koran. Second, the time order of events in the hadith has to be correct. Third, people who have narrated the hadith have to have a reputation for trustworthiness. Fourth, the hadith cannot contradict logic (it can contradict natural laws to show the intervention of the supernatural).

The hadith that has become the source of the "greater Jihad" does not satisfy any of the above-mentioned requirements. It contradicts the definition of Jihad given by the Koran, stated in the authentic hadith collections and demonstrated by the words and deeds of Mohammed. People like Yahya Bin Yala'a and Laith, the narrators of this hadith, are not trusted by Muslim scholars because they are notorious for being liars. This hadith also fails the test of logic because resisting the devil, in Islamic theology, is the beginning step to fulfill what Allah expects Muslims to do, not the ultimate goal. Since jihad against unbelievers is the most important duty upon Muslims, it does not make any sense that the "greater jihad" serves the "smaller jihad." Eliminating temptations that hinder Muslims from obeying Islam and following the example of the Prophet is the preparation for making Jihad. Dr. Sheikh Yusuf al-Qaradawi, who is the most well-known Muslim Scholar living, in a TV program called Al-Fighe wal Hayat (Fiqh and life) explained why the fabricated hadith about the "greater Jihad" is not trusted. He said the only purpose of Jihad is to eliminate non-Muslims from the earth. The Arabic term that he used was "Mahv-ul-kufr-men-al-Arth" which means "wiping Kufr (non-Islamic beliefs) off the earth. Sheikh Yusuf al-Qaradawi emphasized that "Jihad is a part of Islam if there is any infidel that remains on the earth." What he said is from the Koran Sura 8:39 which is nothing more than waging jihad until there is not any <u>Fitna</u> (non-Islamic-belief) on the earth.

There is a similarity between the way Muslims teach their kids and how Western politicians teach their people. In Muslim communities, for instance, if you ask Muslim kids about the Bible, they would say it is something corrupted without knowing whether the Bible is an island or a type of food to eat. The same applies to those who have been told about the "greater jihad." Most of them do not know what hadith means but try to analyze sophisticated Islamic issues and effectively issue Fatwa about which Jihad is "akbar" (greater) and which one is "asqar" (smaller). However, there is a difference too. The difference is that Western politicians use media, books, and articles to make this fake hadith so familiar that everybody knows it. But Muslims do it through family, friends, and mosques. They both mislead, but their methods are different.

Dar-ul-Islam and Dar-ul-Harb

<u>Dar-ul-Islam</u> is a term used by Muslim Scholars for the territory under the political and legal control of Islam. It means, "The House of Peace." <u>Dar-ul-Harb</u> is a term used by Muslim scholars for territory under the control of non-Muslims. It literally means "the House of War." Based on Sharia, every Muslim is obligated to fight until all territories become Dar-ul-Islam. To achieve this goal, Muslim scholars have classified the necessity of Jihad as <u>Fard Ayn</u> meaning a duty that every Muslim who is able must accomplish and <u>Fard Kifaya</u> a duty that is considered fulfilled when enough members of

the Muslim Umma undertake it to ensure it will be accomplished successfully.

Fard is an Arabic word and it means a compulsory obligation and Ayn means present. Fard Ayn is an obligation upon all Muslims and so the fact that some Muslims perform it does not remove the obligation from other Muslims. For example, prayer in Islam is Ayn. All Muslims have to perform it. Praying by some Muslims does not free other Muslims of the obligation of prayer. On the other hand, Fard Kifaya is a communal obligation, so even though it is a duty incumbent on every Muslim, if there are enough Muslims to accomplish that duty, others are not obligated anymore. For example, there is a Muslim's corpse on the ground, if some Muslims take action and bury him or her, it is sufficient so others are not obligated and do not have to participate. Imam Shaffie, another well-known Muslim scholar, said: "A *Fard Kifaya* is a command directed towards everyone seeking only a response from some." Dr. Abdullah Azzam, the author of <u>Defense of The Muslims Lands</u> and one of the most famous Jihadists and a Sharia expert, says that Jihad is Fard Ayn and a type of obligation which is upon every Muslim regardless of whether other Muslims perform it or not (Azzam). Some, however, believe that Jihad is Fard Kifaya, obligatory for every one until there are sufficient numbers of Muslims to perform the obligation. Jihad is Fard Kifaya when it is an "offensive Jihad." Offensive jihad takes place for the fulfillment of the Koran's command and to maintain Jizya (the tax that Christians, Jews, and Zoroastrians must pay to Muslims to have any rights at all—including the right to life—in Muslim lands). In other words, offensive jihad is Da'awa (calling people to become Muslim) by force. The source for the offensive jihad is Sura 8:39 that states Allah Almighty and Majestic says:

And fight them until there is no more *Fitnah* (disbelief and polytheism: i.e. worshipping others besides Allah) and the religion (worship) will all be for Allah alone (in the whole of the world) . . ." The *Fitnah* means *Shirk* as Ibn Abbas and as

Siddi said: "When the *Kuffar* attack and control a country, the *Ummah* is endangered in its religion and it becomes susceptible to doubt in its belief. Fighting then becomes an obligation to protect the religion, lives, *'Ard (land)* and wealth.

Dr. Azzam states:

Where the *Kuffar* are not gathering to fight the Muslims, the fighting becomes *Fard Kifaya* with the minimum requirement of appointing believers to guard borders, and the sending of an army at least once a year to terrorize the enemies of Allah. It is a duty upon the Imam to assemble and send out an army unit into the land of war once or twice every year. Moreover, it is the responsibility of the Muslim population to assist him, and if he does not send an army he is in sin (Azzam).

In "defensive Jihad" the condition is different. In defensive jihad the obligation becomes Fard Ayn. It is a compulsory duty upon everybody. The engagement of all Muslims is necessary. About defensive jihad, Dr. Azzam argues that

This is expelling the *Kuffar* from our land, and it is *Fard Ayn*, a compulsory duty upon all. It is the most important of the compulsory duties and arises in the following conditions: A) If the *Kuffar* enter a land of the Muslims. B) If the rows meet in battle and they begin to approach each other. C) If the Imam calls a person or a people to march forward then they must march. D) If the *Kuffar* capture and imprison a group of Muslims.

All four main Sunni Islamic schools agree that in the above four conditions, Jihad becomes Fard Ayn, a duty upon all Muslims (Azzam). Muslims believe that Israel has been occupied by non-Muslims so Jihad is Fard Ayn and obligatory for all Muslims. Muslims count Israel as a part of Muslims' territory, so they believe that their attacks against Israelis are defending Dar-ul-Islam. And because the United States is one of Israel's allies, Muslims are obligated to wage an obligatory (Fard Ayn) Jihad against America as well. Muslim scholars argue that since the Koran has made it clear that Muslims have to fight until there are no non-Muslims on the earth, the first step of accomplishing this overall goal is to clear all non-Muslims out of Israel, which is in the very heart of Dar-ul-Islam. By the same analogy, many Muslims from all around the world went to Afghanistan to fight against the Soviet Union in the 1980s. They believed that the occupation of Afghanistan by "Communists" had obligated them to wage Jihad to send non-Muslims out of Dar-ul-Islam. Today the same Jihad is going on in Afghanistan for the same reason.

Jihadists blame those Muslims who do not participate in Jihad for not performing an obligatory duty. They say that even if the obligation for Jihad was only Fard Kifaya, if Muslims need more fighters to achieve victory than those who have so far volunteered, those Muslims who have not joined the Jihad are committing sin—failing to fulfill what Allah has commanded them to do. Jihadists count those Muslims who do not engage in fighting against infidels, as friends of the non-Muslims against whom the faithful Muslims must fight as well. When Jihadists attacked the Twin Towers, some Muslims also got killed. Jihadist did not blame themselves for killing them. They refer to Sura 8:73 of Koran that states:

> And those who disbelieve are allies to one another, (and) if you (Muslims of the whole world collectively) do not do so (i.e. become allies, as one united block with one *Khalif*—chief Muslim ruler for the whole Muslim world—to make victorious Allah's religion of Islamic Monotheism) there will be *Fitnah* (wars, battles, polytheism, etc.) and oppression on earth, and a great mischief and corruption (appearance of polytheism).

Jihadists apply this verse to those Muslims who were working in the World Trade Center and got killed. Those Muslims who got killed in the 9/11 attack were either working sincerely to serve the United States or had penetrated into the U.S to help Islam to achieve its goal which is dominating the world. Based on Islamic belief, those who served the United States sincerely are the allies of non-Muslims who need to be killed and those who had penetrated the U.S system to help Islam to achieve its goal are martyrs.

Chapter Six

Different Attitudes Toward Jihad Among Muslims Who Live in the West

Practicing Muslims who live in the West have different ideas about performing Jihad. Even though there is a consensus among all of them that they should strive hard to establish Allah's rules in both the West and the entire world, some disagree with others about taking violent action to achieve that goal. Real Jihadists, who try to walk on the path of Islam correctly, criticize those Muslims who try to conquer the West by peaceful means. Mohammad Abdus-Salam Faraj explains this difference in his book The Absent Obligation:

> There are some that say that we have to endeavor to hold good professions. For instance, we fill the centres with Muslim doctors and architects and this way the Kufr system will collapse by itself effortlessly, then the Muslim ruler will be

formed. Should a person hear this for the first time he would think that is a figment of his imagination or a joke, but truly there is in the Islamic field the one who philosophizes things in this manner. Such saying, despite having no evidence in the Book of Allah or the Sunnah, our current situation is an obstacle against achieving it. So even if we manage to form Muslim doctors and architects, they will be part of the government as well, and no way will a Muslim personality hold a ministerial post unless he completely takes those in the system as friends and protectors.

Islam has one clear path for the establishment of Sharia and that is Jihad. Jihadists never deny Da'wa (calling people to become Muslims). But in their analysis, bringing people to Islam only through Da'wa is incomplete. Faraj argues:

> As we are tackling this point it is worth answering those who say that in order for Islam to be implemented people must be Muslims. Thus people will accept it and its implementations will not fail. But the person who says so is accusing Islam of being incomplete and incapable without realizing it. This is because this religion is suitable for implementation at all times and everywhere, and is able to rule the Muslims and the disbelievers, the sinner and the pious, the knowledgeable and the ignorant. Besides, if people have been living under kufr laws, how then if they find themselves under Islamic Law that is completely just?

Those who have chosen Da'wa as the only way to make the whole world Muslim have been pejoratively called by Jihadists "the Muslims who love life and hate death." Jihadists refer to an authentic hadith narrated by various Sohah (authentic hadith collectiona) in which Mohammad said: "Your love of life and your hatred for fighting" (Faraj). Sura 2:216 says: "Fighting is prescribed upon you though you dislike it, and it may be that you dislike a thing, which is good for you" which is evidence from the Koran that supports the Jihadist view in terms of conquering the world through jihad not through peaceful ways like Da'wa. Moderate Muslims who claim that through gathering knowledge and peaceful Da'wa they are making Jihad, have no Islamic support for their definition of Jihad. Islam has provided Jihad as an effective tool for "cutting the roots of disbelievers." Sura 9:14 is one of many Koranic verse that command Muslims to fight against non-Muslims. It says, "Fight against them so that Allah will punish them by your hands and humiliate them [He] gives you victory over them and heals the soul of the believing people."

Radical and Moderate Muslims

Is every Muslim a terrorist? This is a very common question I have been asked. Actually it is two questions. First, we need to figure out who is a Muslim, then we can figure out whether or not they are terrorists. To be able to answer the first question properly we need to know the characteristics of a Muslim. Many Americans miss the point that not everybody from the Middle East is necessarily a Muslim. There are many Middle Eastern people from Muslim families who are tired of Islamic beliefs and have become atheists. Some others practice Buddhism, Christianity, or Zoroastrianism. Assuming a Middle Eastern person to be a Muslim without having enough knowledge about him or her is misleading when we also want to label them as "moderate," "secular," "culturally Muslim," "nominal Muslim," "radical," or "fanatic."

To recognize whether someone is a Muslim we need to know if he either 1) practices Islam or 2) affirms with confidence that he is a Muslim. We don't need to worry about the details of what constitutes "practicing Islam" here because the point I want to focus on is that one might not practice Islam at all but still believe in Islam, and therefore actually be a Muslim. There are many Muslims in the United States who drink alcohol, eat pork, and go to strip clubs. They do not fast or pray but if you ask them if they are Muslims they firmly say yes. This is the difference between real Muslims and those who just happen to hail from the Middle East without really believing in Islam.

If this sounds a little confusing, you should know that I am simply applying Islam's own definition for who is a Muslim. The Sharia holds that a person does not stop being a Muslim by disobeying the commands of Islam. So a person who eats pork or fails to pray—and thereby appears to be "non-practicing"—does not stop being a Muslim under Islam's own rules. What terminates your status as a Muslim is to deny any of the essential elements of belief or requirements of practice. For example, to eat pork while admitting that Islam forbids it is simply sin, and that person does not become a non-Muslim. But to deny Islamic sources that forbid pork—without even eating it—is to become a non-Muslim.

Recognizing true Muslims—those who are called "radicals" by Western academia—is many times easier than identifying so-called "moderate Muslims." True Muslims try to walk on the path of their prophet, Mohammad, as the great example. They never miss their prayers, fasting or other Islamic obligations. Their female family members are veiled. They stay away from non-Muslims. They do not accept non-Muslims' invitation for eating. They understand and obey Islamic taboos on acts and behaviors. Growing beards by Muslim men is an easy sign for recognizing them; however it's not the main thing. True Muslims know that the Koran expressly tells Muslims that they need to stay away from unclean things like non-Muslims, dogs, etc. On the other hand, moderate Muslims do not care about obeying all those Islamic limitations. They might drink alcohol, eat pork, have girlfriends, or adopt Western appearance. It is difficult to tell if a moderate Muslim is really a Muslim or not.

Even though the chance that a true Muslim would commit Jihadi acts is much higher than the chance for moderate Muslims, it is difficult to guarantee that those moderate Muslims will never repent from their non-Islamic behavior and wage Jihad. Islamic belief is an internal, spiritual condition more than outward appearance, so how can one be sure that there is not a Jihadi behind that Westernized appearance? Aside from Westernized appearance, behavior, and the extent to which a Muslim obeys Islamic limitations, both true Muslims and so-called moderate Muslims believe that the Koran is the criterion. Moderate Muslims try to teach their kids to follow Islamic rules. The moderate Muslim parents try to hide their non-Islamic acts from their children so as not to discourage them from believing in Islam.

An example would be beneficial to illustrate the stealth role that moderate Muslims could play in supporting Jihadi organizations. After a decade, the situation in Afghanistan is still the same. The West could not defeat the Taliban and Al-Qaeda in that country. Why? The reason is that even though the Taliban are not the majority, other Afghans share an Islamic belief that is virtually the same as the Taliban's, so this Jihadi group can survive. Afghans prefer to support the Taliban rather than American troops who are fighting for "democracy" not for Islamic values. The role of the moderate Muslims in the West is the same as the role of the ordinary Afghans. They prefer to support those who fight to establish Islamic values rather than liberty and freedom. In the bottom of their hearts, moderate Muslims agree with the supremacy of Islam and Sharia over democratic values. Since the purpose of Jihad is to make Islam supreme, moderate Muslims fight the same battle that Jihadists do. The difference is that moderates prefer to be supporters rather than perpetrators, although sometimes they might take action. Sometimes they feel guilty for not being a good Muslim and change their method of thinking to become a true, radical Muslim.

Any Muslim who believes that Islam should reign supreme and also believes that the Muslim community has to do its best to establish Sharia in the whole world is a potential Jihadi. Appearance might not be helpful in the process of recognizing potential Jihadists.

Having a Jihadi beard (a long beard with a trimmed mustache) is not a necessary element of being a Jihadist. For example, Tamarlan Tsarnayov—one of the Boston Marathon Bombers—had a clean-shaven appearance.

First Amendment and Counterterrorism Acts

Aside from how much knowledge one might have about the Constitution, it is reasonable to claim that the Constitution should not be interpreted a way that becomes a device against itself. The philosophy of the Unites States Constitution is to make this country prosperous and a better place to live in. The guaranteed freedom in the Constitution must not be interpreted so broadly that it jeopardizes the safety of the United States citizens. If so, it would contradict its goal which is bringing happiness and safety to the citizens.

Some authors interpret the First Amendment in a way that ties the hands of security system in the War against Terrorism. This way of looking at the First Amendment prevents the government to do any surveillance on ideological or religious groups unless there is strong evidence that proves that criminal activity is going on (Cole, 2002). These authors claim that evidence beyond a probable cause (51% or more likely than not that a crime has been committed) standard is necessary in order to justify targeting an ideological group for surveillance. Here are some questions that are significant to the War against Terrorism

> If a fundamentalist religious group or a militia group is preaching the priority of violence or advocating support for terrorism, when should the FBI be permitted to investigate, and how long and intensively should it continue investigating? If a person or group is involved in violent activity, should the FBI identify and monitor others who share the same ideology? If a group is raising money and sending it to a

politically active foreign group, should the FBI be permitted to investigate? Should the government be able to prohibit all support for a group that engages in both violent and peaceful activities? (Cole, 2002)

In response to the above questions, David Cole believes that there needs to be evidence that shows those individuals or groups are planning criminal activity. In his book, Cole supports the idea that terrorist activities should not be monitored and investigated if they have not started committing a crime. He rejects a "guilt by association intelligence model that presumes that all those who share a particular ideology must be monitored on the chance that they will get involved in criminal activities." Under this interpretation of the First Amendment, members of known Jihadi organizations should not be monitored until they blow up something. This is against the purpose of the Constitution, which is to give happiness and prosperity to its people. It ignores the fact that under U.S. law, panning a crime is a criminal conspiracy that is punishable to the same extent as actually committing the crime. The U. S. Constitution and specifically the First Amendment never guarantee those religious ideas that wage war against U.S citizens. Under the Constitution, freedom of religion does not allow the violation of existing laws.

The mistakes made by Cole is that he categorizes Jihad at the same level with as criticizing government policies. but Jihad is not a political speech issue, it is an issue of advocating and working to violently overthrow the U.S. government. Jihad is against the whole existence of this country and its citizens and those who share the same idea with jihadists are already criminals. Expanding the First Amendment so broadly as to make Jihadi ideas a protected exercise of religion is against the spirit of the Constitution. Cole believes that surveillance over those who share the same ideas with violent groups (Jihadists) is against the First Amendment. Even with surveillance and investigation over these groups the government cannot prevent all terrorist acts, so how would it be if we cripple the FBI by interpreting the Constitution in a way that is neither practical nor wise. How could the FBI know if those who advocate Jihad are preparing to attack or not without having some information about it. Having prior information is necessary in the War against Terrorism. Attacking the Antiterrorism and Patriot Act and arguing those acts are against the Constitution just helps Jihadists to attack with impunity.

Cole is upset with the 1996 Antiterrorism Act and the immigration provisions of the 2001 Patriot Act, because he believes those acts should not focus on ideologies that motivate violent groups. Underestimating motivation in committing crime is wrong. Without motivation, people cannot even get out of their beds. Understanding the motivation that makes jihadists give up their lives for terrorist acts is crucial. This assertion that the FBI should start the investigation when a bomb is about to explode is like letting children do whatever ideas they get in their heads and when they kill somebody because of those ideas, the court system will prosecute them. The chance to stop an explosion is close to zero. Only in Hollywood movies can you stop those attacks, therefore watching over those who share the same ideas with Jihadists is a fundamental step toward better security. Cole narrows the range of surveillance and investigation to those who expressly claim that they want to blow up something somewhere. Jihadists are smart enough not to have a panel discussion about their plans. They were smart enough to deceive the security system and carry out the 9/11 attack, so we should not expect them to reveal their terrorist plans via media. Cole continues by saying:

> An investigation must be narrowly limited to determining whether violent activity is in fact being planned. The government should not extend its attention to an individual without reason to suspect—apart from ideology, ethnicity, and religious belief—that he shares in the criminal plans or activity.

He fails to grasp that the one who shares the Idea of Jihad is the next person in line waiting to be called to launch an attack.

Freedom of Religion and Tolerance in Democratic Countries

Where is the line between hate speech and freedom of speech in the U.S Constitution? Is telling the truth about a religion, hate speech? Does Islam tolerate freedom of speech? These are questions people might ask when they have a good understanding of both Islam and the First Amendment. Tolerance is believed to be one of the most important pillars of democratic countries. People in democratic countries have learned to tolerate other people's values and beliefs. Tolerating other people's religion, values, and culture help the citizens of a democratic country to live in peace.

Another pillar of democracy, which is also significant and needs to be guaranteed by a democratic Constitution, is the freedom of speech. As citizens of a democratic country, people have the right to address the problems they feel might jeopardize their lives and freedoms. Some religions and beliefs do not respect such a freedom and find the freedom of speech to violate their values. How can this problem be solved without sacrificing tolerance and freedom of speech then? Islam presumes any non-Islamic idea to be hate speech toward Muslims. So restricting freedom of speech to fight against hate speech is the first step for denying freedom of speech.

Tolerating other beliefs and religions should not restrict the freedom of speech. Islam in its nature is against free speech. Based on Islamic sources, anyone who makes a statement that insults the Koran, Mohammad, and other Islamic sacred beliefs needs to be punished severely. The range of things that constitute an insult is very broad. In fact, denying Allah and Mohammad as his true messenger or believing in anything that might contradict what Islam teaches is insulting Islam. Believing in any other religion insults Islam, because

Sharia says that Mohammad's message is for all people at all times. On the other hand, citizens of a democratic country like the United States want to exercise their right of freedom of speech. Whose expectation of the First Amendment is legitimate? P.J. Vatikiotis in an article called "The Spread of Islamic Terrorism" illustrates how Islamic rules and beliefs are incompatible with democratic societies. He argues:

> If those who claim to represent Islam and wish to implement its law reject all other forms of law, if they insist on the necessity of an all-embracing and uniform ideological purity, there is clearly an unbridgeable gap between them and different social and political conceptions. The dichotomy, in fact, between the Islamic and all other systems of government and authority is clear, sharp, and permanent (Netanyahu).

Freedom of religion in the United States Constitution is expressed in general terms and seems to apply to all religions without exception. It does not exclude any specific religion from having the opportunity to be exercised. This broad interpretation of freedom of religion without exception seems to be unwise. What if some people believe that, based on their religion, they have been commanded to kill others? Don't the citizens of democratic countries have the right to speak up and ask their rulers to explain how all these contradictions are solved? Islam is a religion that commands its followers to kill non-Muslims. If the followers of Islam have different interpretations of the verses that command Muslims to kill non-Muslims, they have to announce their interpretation and post it in their mosques. Classifying Muslims in two major groups as 1) those who deny the verses of the Koran who command Muslims to kill infidels, and 2) Muslims who believe in those verses. Each mosque needs to express its attitude toward the "killing verses" and post it on the gate wall. If a mosque believes in "killing verses" and it's still having attendants, there is something wrong with the interpretation of the freedom of religion.

When Salman Rushdie wrote the book, "Satanic verses," famous Muslim leaders like Ayatollah Khomeinee, issued a Fatwa about the punishment for those who insult Islamic beliefs. Many Muslims took action to kill Rushdie for analyzing the Koran in a way that Muslim Imams found to be disrespectful.

Chapter Seven

Suicide terrorism

Those who call Jihad attacks in which the attackers themselves get killed "suicide attacks' misinterpret the Islamic concept of "Amalyat-al-Esteshhadia." Amalyat-al-Esteshhadia literally means "the mission with the intent of seeking martyrdom. It is exactly what it claims to be, a mission in which the Jihadist seeks martyrdom while performing it, the Jihadist is not committing suicide. Jihadists are different by motivation. But the motivation for so-called "suicide bombers" is most likely to go to heaven directly without being judged by Allah. The Koran gives a very high place to "Jihad-Fee-Sabeelillah"—martyrdom for the cause of Allah. So those who blow themselves up do not have an earthly motivation. They have been convinced to carry out the mission and get killed if necessary, either by reading the authentic Islamic sources about the heavenly benefits of Jihad-Fee-Sabeelillah, or by being encouraged by those whose knowledge is trusted by the one who becomes a volunteer for such a mission.

Writers who argue that suicide attacks by Jihadists are forbidden in Islam because suicide in not permitted in Islam are wrong. They quote some verses from the Koran that say: "O you who believe . . . do not kill yourself . . .". This verse applies to a normal suicide for the situation in which somebody loses his or her hope to live, it does not apply for Jihadi missions. In fact, losing hope is the sin that makes suicide forbidden, Muslims should never lose faith in Allah—who controls the life and fate of all people—to the point that they feel they must kill themselves. By contrast, the Jihadi, because of his belief in a heavenly reward, is full of hope. Many times in Islamic history Muslims have carried out such Jihadi missions. One of them is the attack we discussed earlier carried out against Kaab Ibn Ashraf, a mission in which the attackers faced death. Mohammad allowed "the killing of oneself by oneself" (Khosrokhavar), which means that if a Muslim can kill one non-Muslim, if he or she gets killed in the process, that is fine.

Seeking martyrdom in Shia Islam is essential. Shia believe "the blood wins not the sword." In other words, they believe that, ultimately, those who are willing to sacrifice their lives for the cause of Islam are winners, not their enemies who might have more sophisticated weapons. If a Muslim fights and wins he gets booty—spoil from those he defeated. If he fights and dies, he gets paradise. Westerners call the suicide bombers crazy and do not try to understand their motivations. One reason that Westerners are not interested in digging up the root of this problem is the materialistic worldview that has dominated Western society. Being superficial has become a normal habit accepted by the majority. The majority of Westerners hate to discuss religion. Therefore, it is hard for them to understand other people's values and beliefs that have nothing to do with material prosperity.

Calling suicide bombers crazy people is an easy approach that helps Western society to pass this problem to the next generation and let them deal with it. Adding another word at the end of the word crazy might help to understand the suicide bombers better. Calling them crazy smart, for instance, is closer to the fact. Because some of those crazy people learned how to deceive a gigantic system like the U.S Security System and kill over 3000 people. The motivation that drives them to Amalyat-al-Esteshhadia (operations seeking martyrdom) is going to heaven as the Koran has promised it to them. Some jihadists like Nidal Malik Hasan who get wounded, not killed, have to face the scale in their judgment day. Hasan falls short of the martyr's reward of paradise because he did not meet the Koran's condition of being killed while he was killing. Based on Islam, everybody, except those who have been killed in Jihad-Fee-Sabelillah (Jihad in the way of Allah) has to be judged by Allah to see if his or her good deeds are more than their bad deeds. Islam teaches that there is a scale in the "Judgment Day" that weighs Muslims deeds. To be able to go to heaven, the scale should show that a Muslim's good deeds outweigh his or her bad deeds. Islam teaches how even Mohammad himself was not sure whether he would go to heaven after his death. So for Muslims who really believe in the Koran, a guaranteed heaven is very encouraging. By the way, only Muslims have a chance of going to heaven. Based on Islamic theology, non-Muslims go directly to hell.

The Media and Jihad

Giving priority to financial and material benefits has become the norm in all aspects of Americans' life. The media walks the same path as everybody else. The media tend to exaggerate the knowledge and expertise of the language and cultural experts they invite to speak. If a guest knows how to greet in seven languages, the talk show host introduces them as someone who is fluent in seven languages. For whatever reason, the media are only interested in pushing their own agenda, they are not interested in actually informing people about the truth behind the security threats we face. This is not healthy. The guests the media invites may be able to ask for directions to the U.S. embassy in Arabic, but that does not mean they understand the classical Arabic used in Islamic sources, or can say anything intelligent and truthful about Islam. Knowing how to say "sayonara" is not enough for one to be called an expert in Japanese language, culture, and religion.

Another problem with the media related to Islam and Jihad is that they assume that anyone who has served in military intelligence in Iraq or Afghanistan is an Islamic expert who knows everything about Islam. The media deludes its audience that if you know what "As-salam alaykum" means you are qualified to analyze the Quran and other Islamic sources. Once I decided to improve my English language listening, so I downloaded some podcast to my iPod. I downloaded some analyses about terrorism from "the International Spy Museum." The host was introducing his guest as a veteran cryptologist who speaks 7 languages. Two of the languages were Arabic and Pashto. It made me wonder why I, as an Iranian who has studied Arabic since the first grade, consider the Arabic language so difficult that I would never claim to be fluent in it. At least 50% of the vocabulary of Farsi—the language of Iran where I grew up—are Arabic words, so even an Iranian who cannot read uses quite a bit of Arabic in his or her daily conversation, but they, also, don't claim that they know Arabic. Aside from Arabic, learning Pashto and five other languages so well that one can analyze the religion and culture of the target countries for security purposes, unassisted, is, if not impossible, at least a task that demands more than a hundred years of study. Why just scratching the surface has become the habit of both speakers and listeners in this country puzzles me. Nobody even bothers to test those types of claims. Learning Arabic as the language of the Quran, for the purpose of truly understanding what Islam teaches, is a lifetime job. To be called an Islamic expert, one must read many tens of thousands of pages of credible Islamic sources, in classical Arabic. This is a difficult task that takes dedication and time. Leaders of Jihadi organizations have typically memorized the Koran by the time they are ten years old, not to mention becoming experts in Islamic history and Shari. To use a metaphor, they have suckled Islamic teaching from their mothers' breast. They have passionately devoted their whole lives to understanding Islam, not to just show up on a TV program and call themselves expert. The Jihadis know Islam by taste, so questioning their understanding of Islam and the Quran is not fair.

Chapter Eight

Evangelical Christians and Islam

There are some Christians who go to Islamic countries to share the Gospel. Not all Islamic countries allow them to do so. Countries like Saudi Arabia do not even let non-Muslims in the city of Mecca. Sharing the Gospel in counties like Iran, Afghanistan, Pakistan, Saudi Arabia, Iraq, Egypt and some other counties with deep Islamic roots, is a quite impossible task. The zeal that some evangelical Christians have to share the Gospel with Muslims takes them to secular-Islamic countries like Turkey. Some others go to the Philippines, Indonesia, and Bangladesh with the hope to bring those people to Christ. By and large, the Muslims who live in secular Islamic countries do not have the true sense of the real Islam. In comparison to more pious countries like Iran and Saudi Arabia, they have abandoned Islamic rules and do not really practice Islam in their daily life.

Christian missionaries try to adapt to the host Islamic country. They also want to live safely. Most of them get fascinated with the Islamic culture and avoid any conflict that might arise in the process of sharing Christianity. One idea that they have come up with to make life in those countries easier is that they claim the Koran teaches pretty much the same ideas as the Bible. During their missionary time, or when they come back to the United States, they write a book about how the Koran accepts Jesus as Messiah. These missionaries are like those media and politicians who are misleading Americans about the teaching of Islam.

Evangelical missionaries never get the real taste of Islam for a number of reasons. First, they live in the secular Islamic countries where the people do not know Islam very well. Second, they are not allowed to go to Islamic centers to study Islam before Mullas. All they know about Islam is whatever they have learned from common Muslims, who themselves do not know Islam well. The Christians who are living in the United States trust whatever the missionaries tell them about Islam. The missionaries are considered credible simply because they have lived in those secular Islamic countries for some time, even decades in some cases. Statements like "the Koran never says that the Bible is corrupted," is one of the mistaken assertions that the missionaries make. This is actually a relatively old mistake for Christians, it goes back, at least, to Abdul-Haqq of the Billy Graham organization. The problem arises because Christians have read the Koran without fully understanding the circumstances that led to particular verses—the asbab-ol-nuzul. Specifically with regard to the idea that the Koran does not expressly say that the Bible is corrupt, the real history of what happened to Mohammad—which is the key to understanding what the Koran actually means—is this. Mohammad's first source of information about Judeo-Christian Scripture was the Jews and heretical Christians in Arabia who had been banished from the Byzantine Empire. The Jews told Mohammad that Jesus was just a man and a prophet. The heretics confirmed this. When Mohammad later encountered real Christians who had the true Scripture, he thought that they had exaggerated and twisted the Bible. This is why the Koran warns them not to "exceed the limits of your religion," which, in Arabic, is literally "don't exaggerate" to claim that Jesus is God or Son of God. Surah 5:77 expressly states:

> Say (O Mohammad): 'O people of the Scripture (Jews and Christians)! Exceed not the limits in your religion (by believing in something) other than the truth, and do not follow the vain desires of people who went astray before and who misled many, and strayed (themselves) from the Right Path.'

When the missionaries write books, they transfer their incomplete knowledge about Islam to other people and make the job of educating others about Islam harder for the poor people who have spent their whole lives learning Islam in the proper way. The proper way requires learning Arabic, the Koran, Hadith, Sunna, Islamic History, the principles of Sharia, Elm-ul-Hadith (hadith science), Islamic philosophy, Islamic texts, etc. It is not an easy job.

Muslims never believed that Jesus was more than a prophet. Sura 5:75 says:

> The Messiah, the son of Mary, was no more than an apostle. Other apostles passed away before him. His mother was a saintly woman. They both ate earthly food.

This is what the Koran teaches them. The Koran calls the people who claim Jesus is God or Son of God, infidels. Sura 5:77 expressly tells Christians not to claim something their Bible does not say, doesn't 5:75 impliedly say that the Bible is incorrect? Suras 9:30 and 5:72 expressly apply the term Moshrek (infidel) to Christians. Christians and Jews are expressly accused of "transgressing beyond bounds," that is, twisting the Bible. Sura 5:78 provides:

Those among the Children of Israel who disbelieved were cursed by the tongue of Dawud (David) and Isa (Jesus), son of Maryam (Mary). That was because they disobeyed (Allah and the Messengers) and were ever transgressing beyond bounds.

Mohammad is saying he knows what the "true Bible" says—Jesus is not God—so Christians who claim the Bible says Jesus is God have corrupted their Bible. The verse is saying that those who claim the Bible says Jesus is God will be cursed from the mouth of David and Jesus. The Koran says those who say Jesus was more than a prophet are lying, and their Bible is a false Bible, it is the result of those lies, it's corrupted. The Koran claims that the real Bible accepts Mohammad as the prophet of Allah.

Whether Christian missionaries understand the Koran does say the Bible is corrupted or not, they mislead Christians when it comes to Islam. Unbiblical methods have been invented by some evangelical missionaries to bring Muslims to Christ. They misinterpret the Koranic verses and show them to Muslims to tell them that the Koran teaches as the Bible does. They think they have found the real meaning of the Koran. They claim that all the Muslim scholars for 1400 years have been mistaken about the Koran. They also step down from true, Biblical, Christian belief to make a deal with Muslims. Bibles are now being produced for Muslims that avoid calling Jesus the Son of God, so as not to offend Muslims. In fact, the words "son" and "father" are completely removed from these Bibles when they refer to God or Jesus. Even though many people might find this a good trick, it is unbiblical. It shows that the Word of God does not have power to persuade a non-Christian, so Christians have to come up with tricks to save others. Some have even gone further and implemented the Idea of Niccolo Machiavelli—the Italian Politician—that 'the end justifies the means." They say because the real goal is bringing others to Christ, we are allowed way to present Jesus any way we want. So not only the media and politicians but also some Christian evangelicals are part of the process of hiding the truth about Islam.

Some youth from Muslim families might never have read the Koran or have only heard about Islam from their parents who may not know much about their religion. These young cultural Muslims have never learned Islam in its proper way. They get surprised when they see the verses of the Koran that command Muslims to wage jihad against non-Muslims. In the course of a discussion, when they get exposed to the Koran, they get surprised. They cannot believe that the Koran says such things. They blame the English translation or might try to cut their relationship with those who have shown them those verses. These people are a part of the community that we know as Muslims. They need to hear the truth, not be deceived and remain ignorant. It is the method of dictators and autocratic governments to block the ways that people might hear the truth. Unfortunately, in democratic countries like the United States this problem exists as well for subjects that are deemed to be politically incorrect.

Christians are not against flesh and blood. Showing love and respect to others, including Muslims, is a command from God. Loving Muslims should not deprive Americans from exercising the blessing of freedom of speech. For example, parents love their children, but this love does not prevent them from addressing their children's wrong beliefs. If their children believe that they are allowed to steal from others, the parents search to find out where their children have gotten this idea and then discredit it by showing them the correct way of thinking. Covering up the problem not only does not solve it but also makes it more difficult for others to find a solution for the problem in the coming years. Looking at temporal benefits and passing the problem to the future is equal to ruining the next generation's lives. If people do not stand for the truth today, the next generation thinks that those values are not worth defending. Muslims ought to be loved not more and not less than Hindus or Jews. But if a Muslim believes in something that costs other people's lives, their belief needs to be criticized and this criticism should not be interpreted as hate toward them. They need to learn how to hear other people's criticism about their belief without necessarily killing them. It is neither fair nor wise to pretend that Islam is the religion of peace and not listen to the truth about it. It is also against how Americans have stood for the truth throughout history. That's why the Statue of Liberty was dedicated by the people of France to America as a sign of appreciation for teaching them how they should stand for freedom. Freedom of speech applies to the religion of Islam just as much as it does to any other subject. Americans cannot forget about the valuable blessing of freedom of speech. Muslims have to learn that their response to a logical criticism should not be violence. To the extent that they believe their book to be flawless and think that any criticism requires a violent response, they cannot assimilate into a democratic country like the United States. Muslims need to know that there are other ways to go to heaven without necessarily killing others.

Many Muslims' have learned their understanding of Islam either from their parents, the Imams of their mosques, or the media. They have learned to refer to their Imams for answers to their questions about Islam or issues that relate to religion. For instance, when Christian missionaries tell them the Koran never says the Bible is corrupted, they go to check that claim with their Imam. Normally whatever the Imam says about the Koran's view toward the Bible is more acceptable to the Muslim youth than what Christian missionaries present. Surprisingly, Christian missionaries think that they have discovered things in the Koran that Muslim scholars could not see throughout all of Islamic history. Christian missionaries' underestimate Muslim scholars'

knowledge in Islamic matters. They give more value to Muslims who interpret Islam the same way that they do, although this interpretation cannot be supported with evidence from credible Islamic sources. The moral principles of Islam and Christianity are different, so trying to find a common moral basis—or just assuming a common basis exists—is a mistake. Their gods' characteristics are polar opposite. One has provided a free way to heaven while the other one made martyrdom the only guaranteed way to escape judgment and go to heaven. Attempting to create similarities between Islam and Christianity springs from the desire to see more people come to Christ. This desire leads Christian missionaries to legitimize even unbiblical tricks to get more converts. This method of interpreting the verses of the Koran in such a way that they might look consistent with the Bible has two results: 1) It prevents Christians from knowing the truth about Islam and 2) The Muslim converts become a new type of Christian who believes the Koran is also a book from the same God who gave the Bible to Christians. In other words, it goes to establish a new heresy. Transparency in dealing with Islamic belief is beneficial for both Muslims and non-Muslims. It makes Muslims realize that Westerners understand Islam and Jihad and will never tolerate the idea of killing others for their belief in a different God. In addition, it enables non-Muslims to distinguish between those Muslims who are really dangerous and others who do not want to perform all the commands that have been given in the Koran. The first step toward this transparency is to ask mosques and Islamic centers to publicly announce their interpretation of Sura 9:29. They need to explain whether all the verses of Koran are valid for today and need to be exercised or not. Avoiding answering the above questions directly and without ambiguity could be counted as a sign of deception. The belief that all the verses of the Koran are an integral part of Islamic faith, that the Koran is a book from Allah that is valid until the Last Day, and that Muslims must follow every bit of the Koran makes an unbridgeable gap between Islamic ideas and democracy.

Without transparency, how could Americans be sure that the Muslims who are living in their neighborhoods are not a potential threat to their families. Americans need to see and hear from the Islamic community that Sura 9:29 is not a part of their beliefs. This is a legitimate demand. Muslims need to initiate such transparency. It is not enough to condemn terroristic attacks or to embrace some abrogated parts of the Koran to show that they are peaceful. If Muslims want to condemn Jihadi attacks, they need to reject Sura 9:29. This rejection is the acid test and draws a line between them and the so-called radicals. A Muslim cannot be peaceful and believe in this Sura.

Love is the only way that people can live peacefully in a society. Human beings need to understand that killing others cannot give them eternal life. Jihad is the wrong way of going to heaven. Heaven is a free gift from God. God has prepared the way to heaven through his Son Jesus Christ. If somebody really cares about going to heaven, God has done it for free. "Love your neighbor as yourself" is what followers of God have been commanded. Jesus has already paid the price for those who believe in Him. Muslims need to open their hearts and let Him come in to change their lives. The moment they open their hearts to the truth and let it in, they will realize that there is no place for Jihadists in heaven.

Interpreting Jihad as just fighting against evil temptation is a fabricated idea that precludes people from having a correct understanding of Islam. This book already disproved the idea of the greater jihad. The correct understanding of Islam recognizes that Islam is goal driven, and that its most important goal is to make the religion of Allah reign supreme. All Islamic practices—prayer, fasting, paying zakat, the primary purpose of which is to fund Jihad, and everything else are intended to prepare Muslims to achieve the most important goal. All Muslims are not necessarily aware or feel that they are a part of this mechanism. Some of them might think that they are just practicing their religion, but Islam has already managed all the practices in a way that helps the religion of Allah to become the only allowed religion. Christian missionaries fail to grasp that a Muslim who is nice but believes in the whole Koran, including 9:29, and obeys his or her Imam is no different than a Jihadi. There is no difference between a person who commits an act and a person who agrees the act should be committed. So it really does not make a difference if such a person is either nice or mean.

Apostasy

Muslims are not free to choose any religion other than Islam. If a person's father is a Muslim, under Sharia law he or she is automatically a Muslim. Those whose fathers are Muslim have to be Muslim and remain faithful to the religion of Islam forever. Converting from Islam to any other religion or ideology is prohibited. The Koran, in Sura 5:54, states that Allah will bring Muslim believers, whom he loves, to fight against those who turn away from Islam. Sura 47:25 also calls the people who turn away from Islam "the followers of devil." Sharia law provides four punishments for apostasy. The first punishment is to kill the apostate by hanging. Nowadays in Islamic countries that enforce the Sharia system law system, this punishment is used for men. The second punishment provided by Sharia law is crucifixion but this has been replaced by execution by hanging. The third punishment provided by Sharia is to cut the right hand and the left leg. The last way of punishing an apostate is by exile, which is the punishment for apostate women. The moment a Muslim turns away from Islam, he or she forfeits ownership of all their property. Apostasy also dissolves the marriage relationship between a husband and wife. The apostate parent loses custody of his or her children. Islamic countries that do not enforce Sharia are not necessarily a safe place for an apostate. In Pakistan, Muslims attacked the police station and dragged an apostate to the street and killed him. In Turkey, some young Muslims attacked some Muslim converts and stabbed them to death. Nowadays in Sharia-based countries, the authorities try to kill apostates in a way that looks like an accident. When human rights organizations inform the whole world about an apostate who is under an execution order in an Islamic country, the authorities might release the apostate but then send an agent in an eighteen-wheeler truck to run over the apostate to make it look like an accident. One of the missions of Jihadists always has been is to kill apostates. The philosophy behind killing an apostate is to keep the population of Muslims high and discourage Muslims from turning away from Islam.

Conclusion

People in the West avoid getting into deep and thorough discussions about religion and politics. The reason might be that thy find them controversial. But Islam, as the second largest religion in the world and the fastest growing religion in the United States, has made Americans curious to learn about the idea that is going to change the future of their country.

Analyzing human beings is a very difficult task. Human being's minds are so complicated. They might act differently even every moment. Today a person is law abiding and tomorrow becomes a law breaker. For fifty years somebody might have done nothing wrong but one day he or she does something horrible nobody can imagine. Claiming that Muslims in general are peaceful or violent is misleading. One Muslim is as different from another as one Christian is different from another Christian. Siblings in the same family might be totally different in their personalities. No science can anticipate accurately how a person will react in the future. Muslims are not exceptions. A Muslim woman might wear hijab without believing in Islam. She might wear hijab just because her male family members force her. In contrast, a Muslim woman might dress like a Western woman but think and believe the way that Jihadists do. In a discussion about Islam, a woman with hijab might agree that her religion has commanded many things that should not be followed, but a Muslim woman with Western appearance might stick to thousands of fallacies to justify polygamy and stoning. Even though it is right to think that women with hijab should be stronger in their Islamic belief, it is not a rule without exception. A Muslim man might behave like a Westerner and even drink alcohol and eat pork but he might become a jihadist and this change can happen very suddenly. A Muslim man with a Jihadi beard might never engage in Jihad or try to harm others. No psychiatrist on the planet could anticipate that another psychiatrist would open fire and kill 13 people. The Fort Hood army psychiatrist lived as a nice citizen for over forty years. People testified that he was such a nice person. Nobody ever imagined that one day he would stand for his belief and jeopardize his and other people's lives. These are some of the reasons that this book focused on analyzing Islam rather than considering subjects like whether Muslims are peaceful or violent. Unlike trying to make guesses about individual Muslims, analyzing Islam, based on its authentic sources, leads us to the conclusion that Islam is not the religion of peace if we define peace as living together with respect for others ideas about God and tolerating other people's behavior as far as they do not harm others. Islam defines peace differently. Following Islam and obeying Sharia is the foundation on which Islam defines peace. A Muslim woman in an Islamic community who wants to dress in a way that looks attractive cannot live in peace. The purpose of Islamic dress for women is specifically to hide any physical characteristic that might be attractive to men. The Koran applies the term peace to those who believe in Allah and Mohammad and obey Islamic rules.

To find out if a Muslim is a potential Jihadi or not, the security system either has to have a mind reading machine or conduct surveillance over the communications of suspected people. Defining freedom in a way that handicaps the security system is wrong and jeopardizes citizens' lives. People have appointed the government to defend their safety, freedom, and property. Interpreting the freedom of religion too broadly so as to allow some people to misuse it and plot against people's lives is against the spirit of the U.S Constitution.

Learning classical Arabic, the Koran, hadith, Islamic history, and Mohammad's life are the beginning of knowing Islam. After learning all this, one has to learn how to harmonize all the verses and hadiths that look contradictory. It is not an easy task to distinguish fake hadiths from the authentic hadiths. One who is not expert in the science of Koran and hadith gets confused easily. Understanding Sharia to be able to apply Islamic rules to daily life is even more sophisticated. The problem with many books written about Islam in English is that they just repeat the year that Mohammad was born and his immigration over and over again without clearly answering the questions that have caused confusion about Islam in the West.

Many Muslim scholars, like Sayed Qutb who is respected by hundreds of millions of Muslims, have been criticized as radicals whose ideas are against true Islam. This book has examined the books written by scholars like Ibn Taymyya, Sayed Qutb, Yusuf Qaradawi, Abdullah Azzam, and Mohammad Abdus Salam Faraj and has compared their sources and analogies to show that what they say is simply what the Koran teaches. They thoroughly discuss Islamic subjects and avoid using fallacy to persuade their audiences because they are sure that their analogies are supported by the Koran, Hadith, and Sharia. Most of the people who call these famous scholars radical have never read the read the whole Koran even once, whereas those so-called radicals—famous Muslim scholars—have memorized the whole Koran before age ten. It is unfair to call somebody who never read the most important Islamic book an Islamic expert and call the famous Muslim scholars radicals.

No authenticated Islamic sources endorse the idea of the "greater Jihad." The narrators of the hadith and the book in which it is mentioned are not trusted by Muslim scholars. The concept of a "greater Jihad" also contradicts the Koran's definition of Jihad. The idea of the "greater Jihad" is from a fake hadith. An example of a fake hadith is like when a grocery store bribes a Mullah to narrate a hadith from Mohammad that whoever eats 2 pounds of onions every day will go to heaven. The idea of the "greater Jihad" was fabricated by those who wanted to justify their fear of real Jihad and has found much support by those who thought the idea of a "greater jihad" would be a good scheme to discourage Muslims from waging Jihad. Even though it is good to tell Jihadists that killing others is not accepted by the Creator of the universe, people have the right to hear the truth. Deciding what is good for the U.S citizens to know and how they need to hear it insults their capability to analyze issues.

There are potential Jihadists living in this country who are plotting against others' lives. What encourages them to wage Jihad is Islamic teaching. Those Muslims who believe in Islam and the Koran and understand its teachings about Jihad and believe in it are potential Jihadists who are dangerous. Although they might drink alcohol, eat pork, or dress like Westerners, they might suddenly repent from all those non-Islamic actions and launch a Jihadi attack in the cause of Allah. One might ask how a Muslim with strong belief might commit such non-Islamic acts like eating pork or drinking alcohol. The answer is that they know that those acts are sinful and when other Muslims encourage them to stop those non-Islamic acts, they repent and start to follow Islamic rules. Not all moderate Muslims who have become Westernized are potential JIhadis, but those Muslims who believe in the whole Koran, including 9:29, are potential Jihadis, even if for some years they have fallen into non-Islamic acts. At anytime they might start to become practicing Muslims and support Islam to achieve its goal, which is establishing Sharia in the whole world through Jihad.

GLOSSARY

Abu Backr: The first Islamic caliph

Ahl-Ul-Kitab: Muslims call Christians and Jews, the people of the scripture

Ali ibn Abeetalib: The fourth Muslim caliph

Apostasy: Turning away from Islam

Anwar Sadat: The Egyptian president who got assassinated by an army officer called Khalid Islambulli

Ayesha: Mohammad's wife and Abu Backr's daughter

Beihagi: An Islamic historian

Bukhari: The collector of the most important collection hadith

Caliph: Mohammad's successor

Da'wa: Calling people to become Muslims

Dar-Ul-Harb: The territory of non-Muslims

Dar-Ul-Islam: The territory of Muslims

Dzhokhar Tsarnaev: One of the Boston Marathon bombers

Fatwa: Legal ruling

Fitna: Any non-Islamic belief

Five Pillars: Some Islamic practices including 1) belief 2) praying 3) fasting 4) zakat 5) pilgrimage to Mecca

Hadith: The second most important Islamic source next to the Koran

Hafizun: Those who have memorized the whole Koran

Hasan: The fourth caliph's oldest son

Hilal: whatever is permitted in Islam

Hosain: The fourth caliph's younger son who got killed in Karbala

Ibn Taymeyya: A famous Muslim scholar who was born in Syria in the Mongolian era

Jihad-Fee-Sabeelillah: fighting for the cause of Allah

Jizya: An extra tax that the people of the scripture have to give to Islamic government to be able to have any rights, including the right to life.

Kafir: An Islamic term for non-Muslims

Kufr: Blasphemy

Madinan: Verses revealed to Mohammad when he emigrated to Medina

Mahdee: Muslims' Messiah

Meccan: verses revealed to Mohammad while he was still in Mecca

Mofassereen: The experts who are qualified to interpret the Koran and other important Islamic sources

Moshrik: An Arabic term for idol worshippers

Muhajireen: Those who emigrated for the cause of Allah

Mulla: Muslim religious leaders

Mustafa Azzam: He was a famous jihadi who got assassinated along with his two sons in Pakistan.

Nikab: A type of hijab that covers the face as well as other parts of a Muslim woman's body

Omar: The second caliph and Mohammad's father-in-law

Quraish: The Most important pre-Islamic tribe in Mecca, Mohammad was also from Quraish

Sahih: Literally means correct, it is also the name of the most important hadith collections. Certified to have the highest ranking of authenticity in hadith classification.

Sharia Law: The rules for every aspect of life under Islam

Shia: It is a sect of Islam. They mostly live in Iran, Iraq, Bahrain, and Lebanon

Sheikh: It is an Arabic term for Muslim scholars

Sira: The way that Mohammad lived that is considered as the best example for Muslims

Sohah: The plural of saheeh

Sunan Abu Dawood: It is one of the six important hadith collections

Sunni: It is the main sect of Islam that has more than one billion followers

Sura: Each chapter of the Koran is called a Sura

Umma: the Islamic community of believers

Usul-Al-Figh: The principle of Islamic jurisprudence

Taqiya: Hiding a truth that might hurt Islam's goal

Wahabee: A branch of Sunnis that along with Salafees have the right understanding of Islam and the Koran

Yusuf Al-Qaradawi: The most famous living Sunni scholar

Zohd: It is a book written by Beyhaqee in which the weak hadith of the "greater Jihad" has been discussed.

Bibliography

Alison, G. & Myers, J.J. (2004). *Nuclear Terrorism, the Ultimate Preventable Catastrophe.* Retrieved from Jstore

Azzam, M. *Defense of the Muslim Lands the First Obligation After Iman.* Unknown Publication

Cole, D & Dempsey, J. X. (2006). *Terrorism and the Constitution.* New York: New Press

Combs, C. C. (1997). *Terrorism in the Twenty-First Century.* New Jersey: Simon & Schuster Publication

Dashti, A. (1994). *Twenty Three Years.* California: Mazda Publications

Faraj, M. A. (2000). *The Absent Obligation.* London: Maktabh Al Ansar Publications

Hacker, F.J. (1976). *Crusaders, Criminals, Crazies, Terror and Terrorism in Our Time.* New York: W.W.Norton & Company. Inc.

Keller, N. M. (1994). *Al-Maqasid, Nawawi's Manual of Islam.* Turkey: Amana Publications

Keller, N. M. (2011). *Reliance of the Traveller.* Beltsville, MA, Amana Publications

Khan, M. M. (1997). *Sahih Al-Bukhari.* Riyadh, Saudi Arabia: Darussalam Publications & Distributors

Khosrokhavar, F. (2009). *Inside Jihadism, understanding Jihadi Movements worldwide*. London: Paradigm Publishers

Moghaddam, F. M. *The Staircase to Terrorism, A Psychological Exploration*. Georgetown University. Retrieved from Jstore

Nacos, B. L. (1994). *Terrorism and the Media*. New York: Columbia University Press

Netanyahu, B. (1987). *Terrorism, How the West Can Win*. New York: Avon Publications

Tabari, A. J. (1987). *The History of Al-Tabari Volume VII*. New York: State University of New York Press

www.ingramcontent.com/pod-product-compliance
Ingram Content Group UK Ltd.
Pitfield, Milton Keynes, MK11 3LW, UK
UKHW041958230426
12048UKWH00008B/407